INTERNATIONAL DEVELOPMENT IN FOCUS

Getting Out of School and into the Workplace

Strengthening Work-Based Learning in Upper Secondary Technical Education in Poland's Świętokrzyskie Region

Margo Hoftijzer, Piotr Stronkowski, and Jakub Rozenbaum

WORLD BANK GROUP

Contents

Acknowledgments   *vii*
About the Authors   *ix*
Executive Summary   *xi*
Abbreviations   *xvii*

CHAPTER 1:   **Introduction   1**
Context   1
Objectives   4
Methodology   5
Notes   7
References   7

CHAPTER 2:   **Background   9**
VET in Poland's education system   9
Institutions involved in VET provision   11
Management of the VET system   14
Work-based learning in VET   15
Notes   21
References   21

CHAPTER 3:   **Key Dimensions for Improved Work-Based Learning in Technical Education in Świętokrzyskie   23**
Summary: Key dimensions that determine effective work-based learning   23
Priority dimension 1: An appropriate governance and financing framework for WBL   27
Priority dimension 2: Effective mechanisms for stakeholder consultation and coordination   28
Priority dimension 3: Adequate incentives and capacity of VET providers   32
Priority dimension 4: Adequate incentives and capacity of firms   37
Priority dimension 5: Quality assurance mechanisms for WBL   46
Priority dimension 6: A facilitating role for centers for practical training   52
Notes   59
References   59

CHAPTER 4: **Recommendations, Next Steps, and Lessons Learned** **61**

Recommendations for strengthening WBL in technical education in Świętokrzyskie   61

Next steps: The Świętokrzyskie pilot project to strengthen WBL in technical education   65

Lessons learned for strengthening WBL in a school-based VET system   68

Notes   71

References   71

Appendix A: **Stakeholder Consultations**   **73**

Appendix B: **Policy Lessons on Strengthening Work-Based Learning (ETF)**   **77**

Boxes

ES.1   Priority dimensions for strengthening WBL in technical education in Świętokrzyskie   xiii

ES.2   Recommendations for strengthening WBL in technical education in Świętokrzyskie   xiv

ES.3   Lessons learned for strengthening WBL in a school-based VET system   xv

1.1   Work-based learning: Definition and arrangements   2

2.1   Recent educational reforms   10

2.2   Apprenticeships in basic vocational education   16

3.1   Twenty guiding principles for effective WBL   24

3.2   Six priority dimensions for strengthening work-based learning in technical education Świętokrzyskie   25

3.3   Austria—apprenticeship offices   31

3.4   Denmark—local training committees   31

3.5   Strengthening work-based learning in Latvia   35

3.6   Finland—teachers' work placement periods   35

3.7   Increasing the direct benefits of WBL-provision for firms   39

3.8   Austria—sectoral training funds   41

3.9   Germany—implementation guides   42

3.10   Finland—workplace instructor training within the national qualifications framework   42

3.11   Austria—company awards for strong performance in apprenticeships   44

3.12   The Netherlands—firm accreditation by the Cooperation Organisation for Vocational Education, Training, and the Labour Market   49

3.13   Switzerland—the QualiCarte self-evaluation of WBL   49

3.14   Germany—in-company training plans   50

3.15   Denmark—personal educational portfolio   50

3.16   Austria—quality management of apprenticeships through sound monitoring systems   51

3.17   Austria—training alliances   55

3.18   Germany—models of firm collaboration to provide WBL   56

3.19   Denmark—training centers   56

Figures

1.1   Sequence of activities to support the strengthening of WBL implementation   6

2.1   Scheme of Poland's education system (simplified)   10

B2.2.1   Juvenile workers   16

2.2   Location of practical activities in technical education (share of students, 2016)   18

2.3   Location of traineeships in technical education (share of students, 2016)   19

3.1   Stakeholders in the VET system in Świętokrzyskie   29

B3.6.1   An example of planning and implementation of teacher workplace periods by an educational provider   36

B3.7.1   A stylized model of trainee productivity   40

B3.10.1 Criteria for organizing workplace instructor training (excerpt)   43
B3.10.2 Structuring the training process: an example   44
3.2   Building blocks for effective quality assurance of work-based learning   48
3.3   Location of traineeships in technical education (share of students, selected Świętokrzyskie *poviats*)   53
B3.17.1 Forms of training alliances and organizational options   55
3.4   Possible roles of centers for practical training   57

Tables

ES.1   Book outline   xvi
2.1   Characteristics of training in basic vocational and technical schools   12
2.2   Characteristics of two types of practical vocational training schemes in formal VET   17
2.3   Reimbursement for employers in work-based learning arrangements   20
3.1   Key dimensions and challenges in Świętokrzyskie for strengthening WBL in technical education   26
4.1   Addressing key dimensions for strengthening WBL through the pilot project   68
A.1   Regional working group meetings (May–September 2016)   73
A.2   Individual consultations (June–October 2016)   74
A.3   Group workshops on preparation of pilot project proposal (December 2016–January 2017)   74

Acknowledgments

This book was prepared by a core team led by Margo Hoftijzer and comprising Piotr Stronkowski, Jakub Rozenbaum, and Maciej Gruza. The team further benefited from the valuable inputs of Simon Field, the overall guidance from Cristian Aedo (Practice Manager, Education Global Practice) and Christian Bodewig (Program Leader for Inclusive Growth in the European Union), and the support from Piotr Bezman, Agnieszka Boratynska, Barbara Nowakowska, and Adina Vintan. The book also benefited from the inputs of Jasper van Loo of the European Centre for the Development of Vocational Training (CEDEFOP).

The team would like to thank European Commissioner Corina Crețu for initiating the Catching-Up Regions Initiative under which this book was prepared, Minister Jerzy Kwieciński from the Polish Ministry of Economic Development for his invaluable support, and the European Commission's team for outstanding engagement and support, especially Patrick Amblard, Wallis Goelen, Wolfgang Munch, Justyna Podralska, Krystyna Marek, Magdalena Horodyńska, Karolina Tilman, and Szymon Pogorzelski.

The team would also like to thank World Bank colleagues Arup Banerji, Marina Wes, Carlos Pinerua, Paul Kriss, Marcel Ionescu, and Grzegorz Wolszczak for the advice and guidance provided that contributed to the development of this book.

The content of this book is derived from intensive consultations with a variety of stakeholders as part of the technical assistance that the World Bank provided to the Świętokrzyskie region in Poland in 2016/17 under the Catching-Up Regions Initiative. The team is indebted to all counterparts for the support offered in the elaboration of this study, the timely feedback, the excellent collaboration throughout, and their passion for developing their regions and institutions, especially from the Świętokrzyskie Marshal Office: Grzegorz Orawiec and Sylwia Mucha; from the Ministry of Economic Development: Joanna Kościcka-Posiewka, Anna Banaszczyk, Piotr Krasuski, Paweł Zdun, Hanna Kądziela, and Beata Pojawa; from the Ministry of National Education: Jadwiga Parada and Emilia Maciejewska; and from the members of the Świętokrzyskie Working Group on VET: Joanna Żurawka, Renata Antos, Dominik Kraska, Dariusz Dąbrowski, Aleksandra Marcinkowska, Stanisław Piskorek, Małgorzata

Krawczyk-Blicharska, Bogumiła Wyrzykowska, Mariusz Urbański, Marianna Poddębniak, Tomasz Tworek, Marcin Perz, Miłosz Pamuł, Anna Jastrzębska, Czesław Golis, Krzysztof Łysak, Dorota Tekieli-Bisińska, Bartłomiej Zarzycki, Edyta Smolich, Mariusz Majewski, Michał Zubek, Jerzy Krawczyk, Katarzyna Bilska. Lastly, the team would like to thank all other stakeholders in Świętokrzyskie who contributed to the development of this book, including particularly the many representatives of schools, enterprises, and *poviats* that participated in consultations.

About the Authors

Margo Hoftijzer is a Senior Economist in the Education Global Practice of the World Bank. Her work focuses on the alignment of education and training provision with labor and skills demand. Hoftijzer has led the design and implementation of investment and development policy operations focused on improving education and skills development. She has led and contributed to a variety of peer-reviewed publications and studies on education systems, skill demand and forecasting methodologies, and skill constraints to business development. She is the World Bank's representative to the International Advisory Group on Technical and Vocational Education and Training.

Piotr Stronkowski works as an independent consultant and has over 15 years of professional experience in analyses, research, and evaluation in the areas of social integration, labor markets, and education. Since 2008, he has worked in the areas of evaluation and research, conducting public administration projects for government ministries, and central administration and regional authorities. This has included impact assessments on the design and preparation of policies, programs, and legislation. Stronkowski has also worked as a consultant for international institutions, such as the Organisation for Economic Co-operation and Development, the United Nations Development Programme, the World Bank, and the European Commission.

Jakub Rozenbaum works in the Research Department of the Copernicus Science Center in Warsaw, Poland, leading research projects on science education and learning processes. For several years, he was involved in various projects in the field of public policy, focusing on labor markets, education, and cultural and public participation. He was a member of the team responsible for developing the Polish Qualifications Framework and the Integrated Qualifications System, and designed measures for assuring quality of qualifications.

Executive Summary

OBJECTIVES

The potential positive impact of work-based learning on demand-responsive skill development is widely recognized. Work-based learning (WBL), defined as skill acquisition through exposure to and participation in productive work in real workplaces, can contribute substantially to developing the technical and non-technical skills that future workers require to achieve productive careers, and that employers need to meet labor demand. Moreover, as the inclusion of strong WBL elements in VET strengthens the role of employers in training provision, it is also expected to have a positive impact on the overall quality and relevance of VET.

This book aims to fill a knowledge gap on approaches to support the transition from a largely school-based vocational education and training (VET) system, to training provision that incorporates stronger in-firm learning experiences.[1] While ample literature exists describing VET systems that are largely employer-driven and firm-based, these publications tend to focus on countries that have a relatively long history of incorporating work-based learning in training provision, and where more or less mature institutions to support WBL implementation are already embedded in the VET system. However, substantially less information is available on how mostly school-based VET systems, where stakeholders are less familiar with WBL implementation and where effective supporting institutions are largely absent, can best make the transition to a learning approach that incorporates more and better WBL.

Using one of Poland's regions as a case study, this book aims to shed light on the complexities surrounding the process of incorporating stronger WBL elements in VET provision, focusing particularly on practical implementation challenges faced by employers and schools. The findings and recommendations in this book were developed as part of technical assistance that was provided by the World Bank under the Catching-Up Regions Program financed by the European Union, which was implemented in 2016/2017 and which aimed, among others, to strengthen the implementation of WBL in technical education in the Świętokrzyskie region in Poland.

In addition to serving to inform stakeholders in VET provision and WBL in the Świętokrzyskie region and Poland as a whole, the content of this book aims to provide insights and guidance to policy makers and other actors elsewhere. The analytical framework and international approaches included in the book are expected to be applicable and relevant in a variety of contexts where WBL needs to be strengthened. Moreover, the particular challenges and potential solutions that are identified for the Świętokrzyskie region are expected to resonate with stakeholders elsewhere.

Scope and approach

The book focuses on the specific challenges facing employers and schools in the transition from a school-based VET system to training provision that includes stronger elements of work-based learning, and approaches to address these.

The book focuses on strengthening the incidence, duration, and quality of WBL, which are considered mutually enforcing aspects of work-based learning. Whereas data on the incidence and duration of work placements are more readily available than information on the quality and relevance of WBL, the absence of a WBL quality assurance system combined with feedback received during consultations has highlighted that quality is an equally important aspect to address.

The book emphasizes possible interventions to strengthen WBL that can be carried out without reforming the national regulatory and governance framework. While the book does highlight several national-level aspects that constrain WBL implementation, regional-level interventions to strengthen WBL are more extensively discussed.

The book provides extensive examples of international approaches to facilitate WBL implementation. In particular, for each of the aspects that are found to pose a significant constraint to WBL implementation, the book provides various examples of how these challenges are addressed in other (European) countries, and assesses the extent to which these approaches are replicable in the context of the Świętokrzyskie region.

Strengthening work-based learning in the Świętokrzyskie region in Poland

Weaknesses in the quality and relevance of VET, resulting among others from the absence of strong WBL elements in technical education, are found to constrain the growth potential of Poland's Świętokrzyskie region. The lack of demand-responsive training provision is considered to particularly impede several economic sectors ("smart specializations") that have been identified as potential drivers of growth in the region, including the metal and casting industry in which competitiveness is seen to be impeded by difficulties of firms to recruit and retain sufficiently skilled labor.

The incidence, duration, and quality of WBL in technical education in Świętokrzyskie, as in Poland as a whole, is limited. Even though the regulatory framework allows a substantial share of training to take place in firms, only just over four percent of students spend time with employers beyond the obligatory four weeks of "traineeship" throughout their three-year training program.

To promote WBL in the region, six priority dimensions are identified that require strengthening, with challenges related to stakeholder incentives and capacity playing a fundamental role in all of these. Based on an analytical framework developed by the European Commission that allows the analysis of a wide range of guiding principles for effective WBL, key aspects that constrain effective WBL in the region have been identified. They relate to elements of the national governance and financing framework; stakeholder consultation and coordination mechanisms; incentives and capacity of employers and VET schools; quality and assurance mechanisms; and the role of Centers for Practical Training (box ES.1). Fundamentally, a lack of incentives and capacity among key stakeholders (VET schools and employers) is found to prevent a significant move away from a supply-driven system to an approach in which employers have a greater say and responsibility in VET provision including, specifically, WBL implementation.

A review of international practices that address the priority dimensions reveals a strong focus on permanent institutional mechanisms to facilitate stakeholder coordination and to support individual stakeholders—especially firms—in WBL implementation. The international examples include a diverse range of institutions and mechanisms to advise, direct, oversee, and sometimes finance WBL implementation. While in countries with a longer history of employer-driven training provision (such as Austria and Germany), support mechanisms have been in existence longer and may be more extensive and varied than in countries where the approach is more recent (like in Norway), a feature shared by nearly all approaches is that these support mechanisms appear to be considered structural elements of the VET system. In other words, rather than being support structures that are required only temporarily until a WBL system is up and running, these mechanisms are considered a structural and integral part of the VET system to assure effective WBL.

International examples on motivating and enabling VET schools to move away from a largely supply-driven approach toward a process where employers play a greater part in WBL and, more broadly, training provisions are scarce. Nevertheless, the concerns and interests of stakeholders that are involved in school-based VET are not necessarily aligned with the promotion of WBL, and therefore providing incentives and support to potentially reluctant stakeholders needs to considered to enable the transition to more firm-based learning processes.

BOX ES.1

Priority dimensions for strengthening WBL in technical education in Świętokrzyskie

1. An appropriate governance and financing framework
2. Effective mechanisms for stakeholder consultation and coordination
3. Adequate incentives and capacity of VET providers
4. Adequate incentives and capacity of firms
5. Quality assurance mechanisms for WBL
6. A facilitating role for Centers for Practical Training (CPT)[a]

a. See "VET in the Poland's Education System" section for a description of Centers for Practical Training.

Based on the contextual analysis and the review of international approaches, a set of recommendations was prepared to strengthen WBL in technical education in the Świętokrzyskie region, with a focus on practical interventions "on the ground." In addition to broad proposals related to the overall approach to promote WBL, recommendations focus on addressing practical implementation challenges faced by employers and schools within the existing regulatory framework (box ES.2).

The recommendations suggest tackling priority dimensions simultaneously, initially applying a pragmatic approach focusing on participation of the most "willing and able" schools and firms. Since priority dimensions are considered to

---

BOX ES.2

Recommendations for strengthening WBL in technical education in Świętokrzyskie

General Recommendations:

1. **Apply a comprehensive approach that simultaneously targets (to the extent possible) all priority dimensions.** As the identified challenges are intertwined and reinforcing, this will contribute to transforming a vicious cycle of constraints into a virtuous cycle of opportunities.

2. **Apply a pragmatic approach and initially facilitate WBL participation of those firms and VET providers that show the highest motivation and a minimum level of capacity.** This will increase the likelihood of being able to showcase early success.

National-level recommendations:

3. **Adapt the VET regulatory framework to clarify regulations, increase incentives, and introduce quality assurance mechanisms.** Clear and increased regulatory requirements for WBL will increase incentives for WBL provision, and strengthened quality assurance mechanisms would promote and support schools and firms to ensure the quality and relevance of in-firm learning.

4. **Adapt the accountability and governance framework to increase incentives for engagement in WBL.** National-level interventions, such as introducing performance-based elements in accountability and financing mechanisms, could provide additional incentives to VET schools to strengthen WBL provision.

Regional-level recommendations:

5. **Initially, investing in promoting coordination between individual schools and firms may be more effective than facilitating higher-level and more strategically oriented regional coordination mechanisms.** This focuses attention on the stakeholders directly responsible for implementation.

6. **Address constraints related to incentives and capacity with a well-balanced package of financial and technical support for all key stakeholders.** This includes well-tailored support to all key implementing actors, taking into account that support requirements during the transition period may need to be different and more intensive than once WBL implementation becomes more established.

7. **Support stakeholders with the implementation of sound quality assurance (QA) mechanisms without creating additional barriers for engaging in WBL.** QA approaches are proposed to take into account available capacity and resources, and should not be so stringent that they discourage firms from engaging in WBL.

8. **Adapt the operating model of Centers of Practical Training to promote their facilitation of WBL and the demand-responsiveness of their training provision.** This would both ensure that CPTs promote (rather than discourage) in-firm learning, and improved the quality and relevance of learning that continues to take place in the Centers.

be mutually enforcing, addressing them (to the extent possible) simultaneously is expected to help create a virtuous circle where advances in one area also spur progress in others. For this particular region, the report also proposes to first focus on stakeholders which are most likely to achieve successful results, while ensuring to include participation of various types of stakeholders which may require different types of support (such as for example both large and smaller firms). The rationale for this approach is that it would catalyze broader enthusiasm and capacity for WBL by showcasing early success.

Based on the recommendations, a project was designed to promote the incidence, duration, and quality of WBL by piloting a variety of approaches to address the identified key constraints, which will also generate lessons learned to inform future interventions. This regional project will target WBL provision to students of technical education as an integral part of the formal VET program, with the ultimate objective of improving the employability of VET graduates. The project aims to generate lessons learned that will serve to inform further interventions to strengthen WBL beyond the project implementation period, including in other regions in Poland. The pilot project will use a competitive grant mechanism to collect and identify viable pilot approaches from applicants (each proposal needs to be supported by at least one enterprise and one school). Successful grant applicants will receive sound technical assistance that will be provided by and financed through the project.

The exercise in Świętokrzyskie has generated lessons learned that are applicable in other contexts where WBL elements will be incorporated in a school-based VET system. In addition to lessons related to preparing a sound analysis of the context for WBL provision prior to embarking on concrete interventions, these relate particularly to the recognition of the importance of effective "change management" when implementing reforms; the requirement to identify and support "WBL champions," and the need to adapt international practices to the local context to ensure their positive impact (box ES.3).

BOX ES.3

Lessons learned for strengthening WBL in a school-based VET system

Analyzing the strengths and challenges for WBL implementation

1. Perform a sound analysis of the strengths and weaknesses of the current context for WBL provision, using a combination of regulatory and literature review and stakeholder consultations

2. Include in the analysis a review of the incentives and constraints for WBL implementation of VET schools and other public sector stakeholder

3. Incentives and capacity of stakeholders may be the crucial underlying determinants of effective WBL implementation.

Designing interventions to promote WBL implementation

4. Recognize that introducing substantial elements of WBL in a largely school-based system entails a significant systems' change which will have strong implications for both VET providers and firms

5. Successful reforms to strengthen WBL may require one or more "champions" to trigger and sustain the process

6. When multiple challenges for WBL implementation exist, they might be mutually enforcing and may therefore be best addressed simultaneously

7. Adapt international approaches to facilitate WBL implementation so that they fit the local context.

OUTLINE OF THE BOOK

Chapter 1 introduces the context and objectives of this book, and summarizes the methodology that was applied to develop its findings and recommendations. Chapter 2 describes how VET fits in the overall education system, as well as the key features of the VET system and WBL in Poland and the Świętokrzyskie region. Chapter 3 elaborates on the priority dimensions for strengthening WBL in the region. For each identified priority dimension, this chapter identifies the key challenges faced by WBL stakeholders; describes international approaches to address these constraints; and highlights whether and how these approaches could be applicable in the Świętokrzyskie region. Chapter 4 summarizes the recommendations for strengthening WBL in the region, describes the pilot project that has been designed to address the majority of these constraints in Świętokrzyskie, and highlights how the experiences in the region can inform similar initiatives elsewhere (see table ES.1).

TABLE ES.1 Book outline

Chapter 1	**Introduction** Context, objectives, and methodology					
Chapter 2	**Background** • VET within Poland's education system • Management of the VET system • Work-based-learning in VET					
Chapter 3	**Priority Dimensions for Improving Work-Based Learning**					
	Priority 1: • Areas for improvement[a]	**Priority 2:** • Areas for improvement • International examples • Applicability	**Priority 3:** • Areas for improvement • International examples • Applicability	**Priority 4:** • Areas for improvement • International examples • Applicability	**Priority 5:** • Areas for improvement • International examples • Applicability	**Priority 6:** • Areas for improvement • International examples • Applicability
Chapter 4	**Recommendations, next steps, and lessons learned** • Recommendations for strengthening WBL in Świętokrzyskie					
	• Next steps: the Świętokrzyskie pilot project to strengthen WBL in technical education • Lessons learned for strengthening WBL in a school-based VET system					

Source: World Bank.
a. Priority 1 relates to the national governance and financing framework, which is not explored in-depth in this book and for which no international examples are included.

NOTE

1. In this book the term "school-based VET" refers to the location where the majority of training is provided. In addition to the *location* of training provision, school-based VET (in Poland and elsewhere) tends to be principally *managed* by schools, rather than by employers.

Abbreviations

AO	Apprenticeship Office
BIBB	*Bundesinstitut fuer Berufsbilding* (Federal Institute for Vocational Education and Training)
CCT	Center for Continuing Training
CEI	Center for Education and Improvement
CPT	Center for Practical Training
CVET	continuing vocational education and training
EC	European Commission
EQAVET	European Quality Assurance in Vocational Education and Training
ERDF	European Regional Development Fund
ESF	European Social Fund
ETF	European Training Foundation
EU	European Union
FNBE	Finnish National Board of Education
HVV	*Horeca Vorming Vlaanderen* (Hospitality Training Flanders)
IVET	initial vocational education and training
MoNE	Ministry of National Education
NQF	National Qualifications Framework
OECD	Organisation for Economic Co-operation and Development
PQF	Polish Qualifications Framework
QA	quality assurance
RCE	Requirements for Continuing Education in Teachers' Working Life Competences
RCTD	Regional Center for Teachers' Development
SBB	*Samenwerkingsorganisatie Beroepsonderwijs Bedrijfsleven* (Cooperation Organization for Vocational Education, Training, and the Labor Market)
SEZ	special economic zone
SME	small and medium enterprises

SOLAS	Further Education and Training Authority
TVET	technical vocational education and training
VEM	Vorarlberg electrical and metal
VET	vocational education and training
VLC	Voluntary Labor Corps
WBL	work-based learning

1 Introduction

CONTEXT

Global context

Worldwide, Vocational Education and Training (VET) is receiving increasing attention, particularly as a potentially useful instrument to address high unemployment rates among youth. With the general two-pronged objective of (on the one hand) improving the employment and earnings potential of VET graduates, and (on the other hand) addressing skill constraints of enterprises, VET is considered as a possible means to improve the alignment of skill supply with demand.

VET systems differ substantially across countries, among others in their design, the share of students that are enrolled in VET compared to those that participate in general education, and the extent to which VET succeeds in preparing graduates for productive careers. For example, the share of students in upper secondary education that are enrolled in VET programs varies from 25 in Hungary and 31 percent in Greece, to 73 percent in the Czech Republic. In Poland, the share was 49 percent in 2014 (Eurostat 2016).

The potential positive impact of work-based learning in VET on developing demand-responsive skills are widely recognized. Despite the substantial differences across countries in the design, scope and performance of VET systems, one concept that appears to be broadly accepted globally relates to the benefits of ensuring that students gain practical experience, not only in school workshop settings, but particularly in real workplaces during their training. WBL is defined as learning that takes place through some combination of observing, undertaking, and reflecting on productive work in real workplaces (Kis 2016). The appeal of WBL is that, when implemented effectively, the technical skills that students acquire through WBL are better aligned with actual labor market skill demand than the skills that are acquired through other learning methods, such as classroom teaching or the provision of practical training in venues that provide work floor simulations. In addition, it is assumed that the "real work-floor experience" of WBL helps equip students with essential non-technical skills (such as the ability to work in teams, problem solving, and communication skills) to an extent that is not achieved through other learning approaches.

Moreover, as the inclusion of strong WBL elements increases the role of employers in VET, it is expected to have a positive impact on the overall quality and relevance of VET provision. WBL can only take place when there is a strong partnership between employers and VET providers, and employer motivation to engage in such a partnership is dependent on the extent to which they consider overall VET provision to meet skill demand. Consequently, only programs which meet employer needs will be able to identify WBL placements for their students. The inclusion of WBL in VET provision, particularly when the WBL elements are an obligatory and relatively substantial part of VET programs, is thus expected to promote the demand-responsiveness of training provision, including by influencing the mix of training provision (in terms of the balance of training supply between different specializations) and its content (e.g., occupational standards and curricula).

Different arrangements for WBL exist, which vary particularly in the scope of employer-based learning and in whether they result in formal qualification. Structured WBL schemes, such as apprenticeships or dual programs, tend to incorporate the most extensive WBL elements and lead to a formal qualifications. In work placements, students spend less time with employers than in structured WBL schemes, but the placements nevertheless may contribute to students' qualifications, for example when they are used a part of school-based VET programs. Finally, informal and non-formal WBL arrangements tend to be less well-defined and do not lead to formal qualifications. (see box 1.1) (Kis 2016).[1] Empirical evidence on the benefits of WBL exists mostly for apprenticeship programs, and has found these to be among the most successful forms

---

Work-based learning: Definition and arrangements

Definition:
Learning that takes place through some combination of observing, undertaking, and reflecting on productive work in real workplaces. It may be paid or unpaid and includes a diversity of arrangements (below).

- *Structured WBL schemes*: Forms of WBL, such as apprenticeships and dual programs, that combine on-the-job and off-the-job components, with equal importance, and typically lead to a formal qualification. Duration, learning outcomes, funding and compensation arrangements are determined through a regulatory framework and there is typically a contract between the learner and the firm.

- *Work placements:* Forms of WBL that usually complement formal education and training programs, that are shorter and less regulated than formal structured WBL schemes. Examples include internships, work shadowing opportunities and other work placements used as part of school-based VET programs.

- *Informal and non-formal WBL:* Forms of WBL that do not lead to a qualification and typically lack explicit targeted learning outcomes. This includes, for example, learning-by doing or learning from managers or co-workers.

Source: Kis 2016.

of VET when measured in terms of labor market outcomes, and the satisfaction of employers with VET provision.

Various countries, particularly in Europe, have well-established VET systems that historically place a lot of emphasis on integrating WBL into education and training provision, particularly in the form of structured WBL schemes such as apprenticeships. Extensive apprenticeship systems as part of initial education and training for young people exist in Austria, Denmark, Germany, the Netherlands, and Switzerland, and in a slightly different form in Norway. The UK also has large numbers of apprentices, although many of them are older incumbent workers pursuing somewhat shorter programs than in other countries. France also maintains a substantial apprentice system. Many other European countries, often on a smaller scale are seeking to develop WBL in the form of apprenticeships. Germany has very well-known and successful apprenticeship arrangements. There, of the 47.8 percent of students in upper secondary education which were enrolled in initial VET in 2014 (corresponding to the EU average), 86.4 percent combined work and school-based programs (which is substantially higher than the EU average of 34 percent), typically spending four days per week in an apprenticeship with the employer and the remaining day in a vocational school. This high level of participation in WBL depends on the support of employers for apprenticeship systems.[2] The German system facilitates a smooth transition from school to the labor market: in 2015, the employment rate of recent graduates was 90.4 percent, again substantially higher than the EU average of 76.9 percent (CEDEFOP 2017).

The relatively sound labor market performance of graduates from VET systems that integrate strong WBL elements, has resulted in a desire to emulate the approach elsewhere. In the European context, for example, the European Commission has developed several publications providing guidance for Member States on strengthening WBL implementation.[3] Another important initiative is the European Alliance for Apprenticeships (EAfA), a platform bringing together governments, business, social partners, chambers, VET providers etc. The main objective of the Alliance is to strengthen cooperation in the field of WBL. Outside of Europe, Singapore and Australia are examples of countries which have successfully introduced strong WBL elements in their VET provision. The topic of WBL is also high on the agenda of the OECD, which underlines the importance of WBL in good quality VET systems (OECD 2014).

In many other countries, especially those where traditional VET provision is largely school-based or where the private sector is unorganized, efforts to strengthen WBL in VET are not always immediately successful. Where VET provision is largely school-based, stakeholders often find it complicated to move from a supply-driven system to an approach where employers play a greater part in determining the occupational mix and content of training provision. Reluctance to reform, vested interests of stakeholders involved in school-based VET provision, and employer apathy, may all create significant obstacles to establishing the kind of partnerships between employers and public vocational programs that might foster effective WBL and overall demand-responsiveness of VET provision, and subsequently improved employment outcomes of VET graduates.

In cases where the school—rather than the employer—remains the principal driver of VET provision, identifying sufficient WBL places in firms tends to be a particular challenge. In countries like Austria, Germany, and Switzerland, students first identify an employer offering an apprenticeship, after which local authorities are required to provide them with a matching place in a vocational school for the school-based elements of their training. In for example Denmark, on the other hand, students first enroll in a VET school, after which an apprenticeship needs to be identified, which can be a challenging task that is not always successful. Countries which aim to incorporate stronger WBL elements in a largely school-based VET system, may choose the "school-first" approach. This is for example the case in Latvia, where a reform is ongoing to strengthen WBL in VET. This could be considered a justifiable option, considering that schools have more experience and capacity for VET provision than employers, and the risk that an exclusive "employer-first" approach may result in a significant disruption in VET delivery that reduces the supply of training possibilities for students. It also entails, however, that in addition to the strong coordination between the employer and the VET school that is in any case required in either approach, coordination also needs to preoccupy itself with the often-difficult task of finding a placement with an employer.

The context in Poland

Poland's initial vocational education system includes two types of schools: basic vocational schools, offering a three-year program, and four-year upper secondary technical schools, which offer access to university. While well over half of students in basic vocational education participate in an apprenticeship scheme, training provision in technical education remains largely school-based (See chapter 2 for a more elaborate description of Poland's education and VET system).

In 2016, the World Bank started providing technical assistance to the self-government of Poland's Świętokrzyskie region, aimed at strengthening the implementation of WBL in technical schools. This support was part of a formal program of collaboration between the Government of Poland, two regional self-governments, the European Commission, and the World Bank to improve the impact of European Union (EU) financing allocated to improve innovation, employment, and economic growth.[4] The regions supported by this "Catching-Up Regions Initiative," Świętokrzyskie and Podkarpackie, participated in the program since structural challenges to economic and employment growth substantially impede their potential to converge toward European averages. The regional government of the Świętokrzyskie region selected the strengthening of WBL in technical schools as one of the priority areas in which the World Bank would provide technical assistance.

During the implementation of the program, which took place during a 10-month period between May, 2016 and March, 2017, the World Bank worked closely with the regional self-government, as well as the national government, the European Commission, and other stakeholders, to pave the way for further interventions that will structurally increase the incidence and effectiveness of WBL, including those that will be financed from EU funds.

OBJECTIVES

This book describes the methodology and the main findings and results of the technical assistance that was provided to the Świętokrzyskie region in Poland to strengthen the incidence, duration, and quality of WBL in upper secondary technical education. In line with the existing policy framework and stakeholder preferences, the assistance focused on strengthening work placements, while assuming that the VET school remains the principal driver of training provision.

The book aims to fill the knowledge gap on feasible approaches to support the transition from a largely school-based VET system, to training provision that incorporates stronger in-firm learning experiences, in a context where neither schools nor firms have substantial experience in WBL implementation. Relatively extensive literature is available on VET systems that are largely employer-driven and firm-based, particularly on those that apply apprenticeship mechanisms. However, considerably less information exists on practices and challenges to the process of incorporating stronger WBL elements in a VET system that still relies mostly on school-based training provision. By using the example of the Świętokrzyskie region as a case study, this book aims to shed some light on the complexities surrounding this transition.

The focus of the book is on addressing practical implementation challenges faced by employers and schools, within the existing regulatory framework. While strengths and challenges of the national regulatory and governance system are broadly identified, the emphasis of the book is on facilitating employers and schools with support "on the ground" through sub-national interventions.

The book aims to provide knowledge and guidance to stakeholders globally. The analytical framework and international approaches described in the book are expected to be applicable and relevant in a variety of contexts where VET systems are in place but where in-firm learning opportunities need to be strengthened. Moreover, it is assumed that the particular challenges and potential solutions that are identified for the Świętokrzyskie region will resonate with stakeholders elsewhere, and that the key recommendations for this particular case study can usefully be taken into account when designing interventions elsewhere.

METHODOLOGY

The approach taken to support WBL implementation consisted of four phases. The first phase comprised the identification of the main strengths and challenges of current WBL implementation in Świętokrzyskie—and to an extent in Poland as a whole. The second phase consisted of a review of practices applied in other countries to address the main challenges that were identified in the preceding analysis, and an assessment of the replicability of these practices in Świętokrzyskie. During the third phase, a program of interventions to strengthen WBL was designed, and approved to be financed by EC funding. The final phase is the implementation of this pilot project, which is expected to take place over 2017–20. In addition, it is proposed that policy makers consider additional identified recommendations to adjust the national regulatory and governance framework regulatory to strengthen the extent to which it promotes WBL. The four phases are illustrated in figure 1.1, and further described below.

The analysis of strengths and weaknesses of WBL in Świętokrzyskie was based on the 2015 European Commission's publication on "20 guiding principles of high-performing apprenticeships and work-based learning"(European Commission 2015). It proposes a framework of 20 measures designed to ensure effective WBL, grouped in four key areas:

FIGURE 1.1

Sequence of activities to support the strengthening of WBL implementation

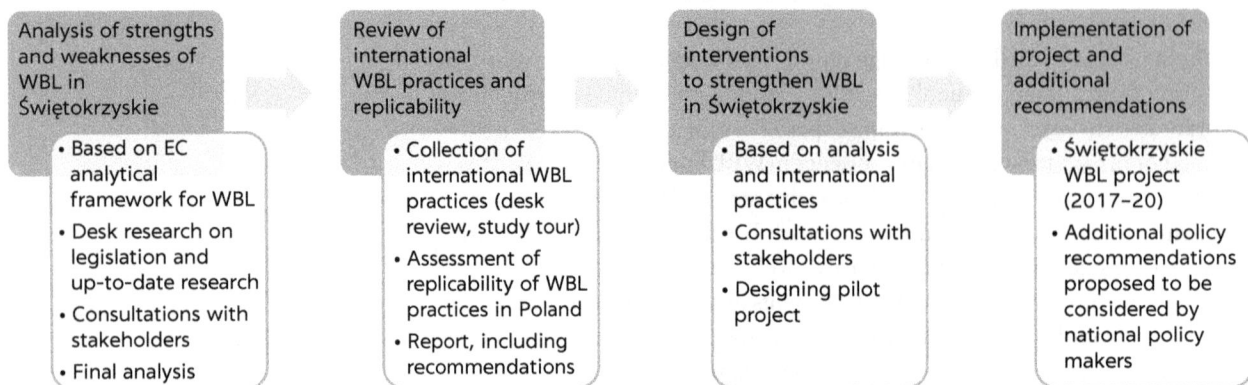

Analysis of strengths and weaknesses of WBL in Świętokrzyskie	Review of international WBL practices and replicability	Design of interventions to strengthen WBL in Świętokrzyskie	Implementation of project and additional recommendations
• Based on EC analytical framework for WBL • Desk research on legislation and up-to-date research • Consultations with stakeholders • Final analysis	• Collection of international WBL practices (desk review, study tour) • Assessment of replicability of WBL practices in Poland • Report, including recommendations	• Based on analysis and international practices • Consultations with stakeholders • Designing pilot project	• Świętokrzyskie WBL project (2017–20) • Additional policy recommendations proposed to be considered by national policy makers

Source: World Bank.
Note: WBL = work-based learning; EC = European Commission.

1. National governance and social partners' involvement
2. Support for companies offering apprenticeships
3. Attractiveness of apprenticeships for students
4. Quality assurance in WBL.

Based on this framework, an analysis was conducted through desk-reviews of relevant regulations and literature, as well as through extensive consultations with key stakeholders, including representatives of VET providers, firms, and local, regional, and national government officials.[5] This effort resulted in an adapted version of the original analytical framework, which captures several dimensions that pose a significant challenge to WBL implementation in the Polish context, but which were not explicitly captured in the original framework. Six key dimensions were distinguished, which refer to some of European Commission's principles, with stress put on slightly different issues. Description of these six key dimensions and their most important features forms the core of this book. Those dimensions are:

1. An appropriate governance and financing framework for VET
2. Effective mechanisms for stakeholder consultation and coordination
3. Adequate incentives and capacity of VET providers
4. Adequate incentives and capacity of employers
5. Quality assurance mechanisms for WBL
6. A facilitating role for Centers for Practical Training.

The review of international WBL practices focused on policies and interventions that address the main identified challenges in the region.[6] The analysis of international practices was based on desk review and supplemented by a stakeholder study visit to Latvia.[7] Practices identified were subsequently analyzed in terms of the possibility of successful replication in the Polish, and particularly the Świętokrzyskie, context.

The design of interventions to strengthen WBL in Świętokrzyskie culminated in the preparation of a regional pilot project proposal to be financed through the European Social Fund as a social innovation. The project is intended to support the piloting of various approaches to strengthening WBL in several municipalities in the region.

Pilot project implementation is scheduled to take place from 2017 to 2020, and is expected to generate lessons learned that can usefully be applied to strengthen WBL in VET in other regions in the country as well as inform policy reforms at the national level.

In addition to the pilot project, a set of recommendations addressed to regional and national authorities were formulated as part of the project. Recommendations were based on the identified challenges and obstacles for implementation of WBL in the Polish context, and focused on the improvement of the regulatory and governance framework, as well as the utilization of EU financing, particularly the European Social Fund.

NOTES

1. As will be further discussed in chapter 2 of this book, work placements are the most common form of WBL in technical education in Poland, whereas both structural WBL arrangements and work placements are applied in basic vocational education.
2. WBL can be offered by both private and public sector employers. As this book focuses on WBL in the private sector, it regularly refers to "firms" and "enterprises" as WBL providers. Many of the challenges to implementing WBL that are described in this book also apply to the public sector; however, approaches to address these (e.g., related to incentives and financing) may vary between the two sectors.
3. See, among others, European Commission (2013) and European Commission (2015).
4. "Administration Agreement between the European Commission and the International Bank for Reconstruction and Development on the Part II Europe 2020 Programmatic Single-Donor Trust Fund" (Trust Fund No. TF072592).
5. See the "References" section and appendix A summarizing the stakeholders who were consulted.
6. The review excluded an in-depth review of practices across Poland. As strong WBL aspects are incorporated in Poland's basic vocational education (see chapter 2), a future review of determinants of successful WBL elements in this VET segment could provide useful insights, in addition to those generated by the review of international practices.
7. Latvia was selected for a study visit since it recently started implementing a comprehensive set of interventions to transition from a VET system that is mostly school-based to one that incorporates strong elements of WBL.

REFERENCES

CEDEFOP. 2017. "On the Way to 2020: Data for Vocational Education and Training Policies. Country Statistical Overviews—2016 Update." Cedefop Research Paper 61. Publications Office, Luxembourg.

European Commission. 2013. *Work-Based Learning in Europe: Practices and Policy Pointers*. European Commission.

——. 2015. *High-Performing Apprenticeships and Work-Based Learning - 20 Guiding Principles*. European Commission, DG Employment.

Eurostat. 2016. *Vocational Education and Training Statistics* (accessed 31 March 2017), http://ec.europa.eu/eurostat/statistics-explained/index.php/Vocational_education_and _training_statistics.

Kis, V. 2016. *Work, Train, Win: Work-Based Learning Design and Management for Productivity Gains*, Paris: OECD Publishing.

OECD. 2014. *Skills beyond Schools. Synthesis Report*. Review of Vocational Education and Training. Paris: OECD publishing.

2 Background
VET AND WBL IN POLAND

VET IN POLAND'S EDUCATION SYSTEM

Structure of Poland's education system

Compulsory education in Poland lasts nine years. It consists of primary education (*szkoła podstawowa*), which principally starts at the age of seven and lasts for six years, and three years of lower secondary education (*gimnazjum*), which usually ends at the age of 16.

Differentiation of educational pathways begins at the upper secondary level. There are four types of education for young graduates of lower secondary education:

1) Three-year upper secondary general education (*liceum*), which ends with the *matura* exam, allowing access to tertiary and post-secondary education

2) Four-year upper secondary technical education (*technikum*), which combines general education on the *liceum* level with vocational education. It ends with both the *matura* exam and the vocational qualification exam, awarding the title of technician

3) Three-year basic vocational education (*zasadnicza szkoła zawodowa*), combining vocational, practical education with basic general education. Two distinct forms of basic vocational education exist, including an apprenticeship scheme for "juvenile workers."[1] It culminates in the vocational qualification exam. It can be supplemented with general secondary school for adults, which—after passing the *matura* exam—then allows access to post-secondary or tertiary education

4) Three-year special needs education preparing for work (*szkoła specjalna przysposabiająca do pracy*), designed for students with learning disabilities. It combines basic general and vocational education, but does not end with a formal qualification.

A simplified scheme including the formal vocational education and training (VET) elements of Poland's education system is depicted in figure 2.1, below. Reforms to this system as announced by the Polish government in 2016, are summarized in box 2.1.

FIGURE 2.1

Scheme of Poland's education system (simplified)

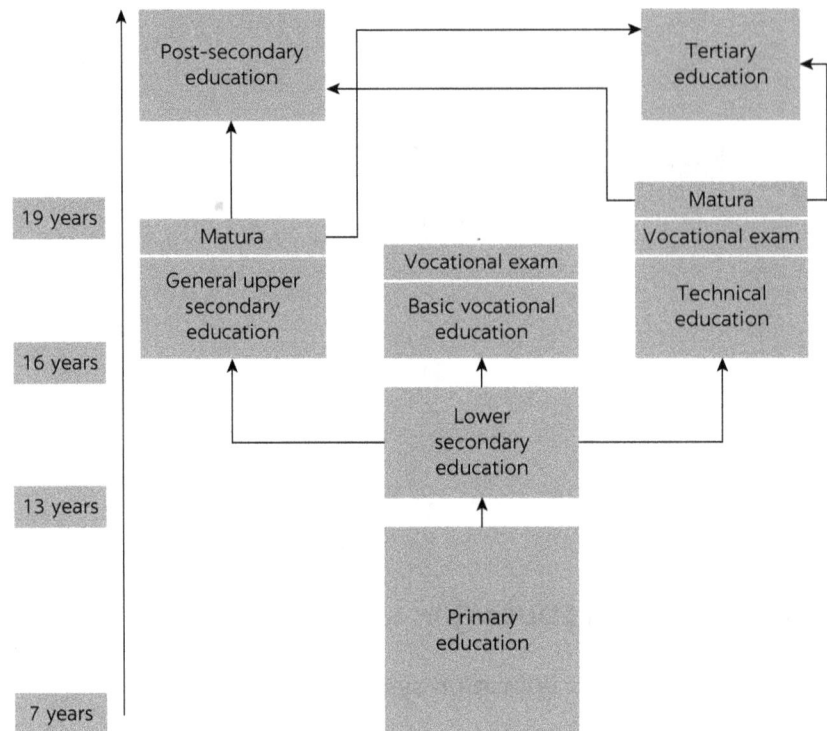

Source: World Bank.

BOX 2.1

Recent educational reforms

In December 2016, the Polish government anounced reforms that were to come into force in the school year 2017/2018. The major aspect of the reform is a change in the structure of the education system: lower secondary education will be eliminated and replaced by an additional two years of primary education, and an extension of the duration of the current upper secondary education by one year. This reform is in fact a return to the structure that was in place before 1999.

As for vocational education and training, two major changes entail:

- The extension of technical education by one year, making it a five-year program
- A change in nomenclature of the current basic vocational schools into "industry schools" (*szkoła branżowa*), and the introduction of a two-years second level program in industry schools, where an additional vocational

qualification, as well as the *matura* diploma might be acquired (the second level industry school program resembles the pre-1999 "supplementary technical school," which served the same purpose).

The law approved in December 2016 does not introduce additional substantial changes in VET that relate to the organization and content of the learning process, including WBL. However, some changes may be introduced in the forthcoming ordinances. The Ministry of National Education has stressed the importance of WBL and the need to strengthen its implementation, and has indicated to aim to address the challenges that are identified and analyzed in this book. The authors of this book therefore assume that, despite forthcoming reforms, the contents of this book remain relevant and may serve as input for further policy decisions on the strengthening of WBL.

Students' interest in different pathways is changing in favor of technical schools. The school year 2015/2016 was the first for 10 years in which enrolment in technical schools was higher than in general secondary school. Specifically, 42.9 percent of youth in upper secondary schools enrolled in technical education, compared to 41.4 percent in general education. The share of students in upper secondary education that were enrolled in basic vocational education in 2015/2016 was 14.8 percent, substantially lower than around 25 years ago when this type of education attracted most students among the various available options. Less than 1 percent of students were enrolled in special needs education.[2] There are significant gender differences in enrolment by education type: females made up 60.1 percent of students in upper secondary general education, but only 41.2 percent and 32.0 percent in technical schools and vocational schools, respectively (Central Statistical Office 2016).

Initial vocational education is organized according to target occupations. The Ministry of National Education (MoNE) publishes lists of occupations that can be provided by VET schools. In 2016, there were 209 occupations in the ministerial classification.[3] Each occupation consists of up to three qualifications that form a consistent set of learning outcomes. The list of learning outcomes for each qualification and occupation forms a core curriculum. VET schools may prepare their own curricula to reflect the needs of local enterprises, as long as it remains consistent with the core curricula. However, the majority of schools prefer to use model curricula, as designed by the National Center for Supporting Vocational and Continuing Education. Although the 2015 Act on the Integrated Qualifications System foresees the establishment a Polish Qualifications Framework (PQF), updated qualifications designed with the input from the private sector remain to be developed.[4]

Beyond secondary education, the Polish system offers post-secondary and tertiary education, and continuing learning programs for adults. Post-secondary vocational schools provide vocational training for holders of the *matura* certificate. At the tertiary level, bachelor and master programs are offered. Continuing learning institutions offer vocational qualification courses, which are free-of-charge and available for all adults regardless of their prior education, and grant officially recognized vocational qualifications.

Each education level (with the exception of tertiary education) ends with an external examination, giving access to another level and/or offering a labor market credential. For upper secondary education, examinations are the general *matura* exam and the vocational qualifications exam, which are managed by the Central Examination Board and its regional counterparts. Schools and other educational institutions organize them on their premises, but the examination board is responsible for the assessment process—preparing the exam questions and tasks, appointing assessors, awarding diplomas.

INSTITUTIONS INVOLVED IN VET PROVISION

The main providers of formal VET are basic vocational schools and technical schools. As indicated above, they provide different types of VET at the upper secondary level, with a main difference that technical education results in a *matura* graduation in addition to a vocational qualification.[5]

TABLE 2.1 **Characteristics of training in basic vocational and technical schools**

DIMENSION	BASIC VOCATIONAL SCHOOL	TECHNICAL SCHOOL
Length of education cycle	3 years	4 years
Student's status	Either student or juvenile worker	Student
Role of school in education process	In the case of students, the school is responsible for the entire learning process	The school is always responsible for the whole process of education
	In the case of juvenile workers, the school is responsible for general education and possibly theoretical vocational training (the employer is responsible for the rest)	
Final external exams	Single vocational qualification exam	*Matura* general exam and up to three vocational qualifications exams (granting the "technician" professional title)
Role of general education	Only supplementary, and on a basic level—it doesn't end with any exam	At least as important as vocational education, and resulting in *matura* exam
Scope of vocational training in the education program	630 school hours of theoretical training (24 percent of curriculum)	735 school hours of theoretical training (18 percent of curriculum)
	970 school hours of practical training (38 percent of curriculum)	735 school hours of "practical activities" (18 percent of curriculum) + from 4 to 12 weeks of "traineeship"[a]

Source: World Bank.
a. See this chapter's section on "Work-Based Learning in VET" for a description of the terms "practical activities" and "traineeship."

Additional differences between basic and technical schools are summarized in table 2.1.

Basic vocational and technical schools can engage other entities in the provision of both theoretical and practical aspects of training. In addition to involving employers in training provision (which will be discussed in detail in the remainder of the book these include the following:

- **Centers for Practical Training** (*Centrum Kształcenia Praktycznego*) are entities whose main purpose is to organize practical vocational training for students from technical education and basic vocational schools—both through training in their own workshops, as well as intermediating between schools and employers in WBL agreements. Centers for Practical Training (CPTs) might also provide continuing vocational training, for example, in the form of vocational qualification courses. They are also entitled to organize vocational qualification exams prepared by examination boards. Currently there are ca. 150 CPTs in Poland—the MoNE's goal is to establish a CPT in each of the country's 380 *poviats*.
- **Centers for Continuing Training** (*Centrum Kształcenia Ustawicznego*) are similar to CPTs, but designed in the first place to provide vocational training for adults in the form of vocational qualification courses (which cover the scope of one qualification) or shorter courses in particular competences. Centers for Continuing Training (CCTs) might also organize practical vocational training for students as a supplementary activity.

- **Centers for Education and Improvement** (*Ośrodek Dokształcania i Doskonalenia Zawodowego*) support other providers, especially basic vocational schools, offering theoretical vocational training, as well as general education for juvenile workers who do not attend school.
- Vocational schools and CPTs, CCTs, and Center for Education and Improvement (CEIs) can form school complexes, which are called **Centers for Vocational and Continuing Training** (*Centrum Kształcenia Zawodowego i Ustawicznego*).

In addition to schools and other entities which provide training, various institutions are responsible for system management and oversight. The main institutions with a mandate in this regard are as follows:

- **The Ministry of National Education** (MoNE) is responsible for creating the legal and financial framework of the VET system. MoNE is responsible for developing the core curriculum; the general principles for the assessments of learning outcomes; and the principles of WBL arrangements. In addition, MoNE is responsible for financing education, including VET.
- **Central and regional examination boards** (*komisje egzaminacyjne*) are institutions supervised by the MoNE and responsible for preparing and managing the process of external examinations—both general (*matura*) and vocational.
- **The educational superintendent** (*kurator oświaty*) is a regional supervising body, supervised by the MoNE, responsible for quality assurance of the learning process.
- **Regional self-government** (i.e., the highest level of self-government structure in Poland) is responsible for establishing a regional educational strategy, including on VET. A principle instrument by which the regional government may influence VET and implement the regional strategy is through EU Funds, managed at the regional level. The regional self-government has no formal authority over poviat self-government (see below); however, it can develop soft measures to coordinate educational policies.[6]
- *Poviat* **self-government** (middle level of self-government structure, or "county") is the founding and managing authority of most public VET providers.[7] The poviat is responsible for organizing upper secondary education through a network of schools and other entities (like CPTs). The poviat allocates funding for education from the national budget to schools, and may add supplementary funds from its own budget. It may influence the type of occupations that are offered in VET schools, as well as the organization of learning processes. There appears to be large variety in the extent to which poviat self-governments make use of their mandate in these areas, including in their engagement in improving the quality and demand-responsiveness of VET.
- **Regional labor market councils** operate on the basis of the Law on Promotion of Employment, and are managed by regional employment offices. A labor market council is a collective body including representatives of the social partners from the region. In the area of education, the council has the mandate to provide advice on schools' proposals to start providing training on new occupations. In some regions, labor market councils are rather inactive and therefore have a relatively limited impact on the local educational system, including on VET.

MANAGEMENT OF THE VET SYSTEM

Management of VET provision

Management of education provision in Poland is decentralized. The Ministry of National Education is responsible for establishing the regulatory framework, developing core curricula and other standards, ensuring financing, and organizing mechanisms for ensuring quality of education (educational superintendents) and the assessment of learning outcomes (external exams). Regional authorities have a responsibility for education strategy as part of their mandate for regional development; beyond the regional labor market councils, however, there appear to be limited instruments at the regional level to carry out such responsibility.

Management of educational institutions is mainly a responsibility of the poviat governments. Poviat governments have direct responsibility for VET, in particular for their establishment and supervision. The poviat government also appoints the head teachers of VET schools. More generally, local authorities are responsible for local educational policy and for coordinating the educational offer to ensure that it meets labor demand. However, the extent to which this occurs in practice differs between *poviats* and depends, among others, on local capacity. Poor communication and coordination mechanisms between authorities, VET providers, and employers, exacerbated by weak labor market information systems, may contribute to overinvestment in some occupations, insufficient relevance of VET, and subsequent labor market mismatches.

Responsibility for education provision is situated on the level of single schools. VET schools propose the occupations that they want to train in and the organization of the training process to the poviat authorities for approval. In circumstances where information on labor market demand is unavailable or not well-incorporated in decision making (such as often appears to be the case in the Świętokrzyskie region), decisions on which occupations to offer appear to be largely driven by the schools' existing capacity and the skills of their teacher workforce, combined with assumptions about which occupations will attract the most students. Financial considerations may also lead schools to offer those occupations which can be provided at relatively low costs. Whereas consultations in the Świętokrzyskie region identified several examples of training provision that was well-geared to labor demand, generally the above factors are assumed to contribute to existing skill mismatches in the region.

Private sector engagement in the management of technical education is limited. On the regional and sub-regional level, formal private sector engagement does not seem to go beyond participation in labor market councils. There is no formal obligation for school councils to include private sector representation; rather, relevant legislation does not refer to the possibility of including any other members in the school council than representatives of teachers, students, and parents.

Financing of VET provision

The financing of secondary education in Poland is based on transfers from the national budget. The budget allocation for each poviat is determined by an algorithm designed by the MoNE which is mostly based on student numbers. The allocation formula does not take into consideration the type of education (general or VET). Thus, poviat authorities receive the same amount for VET students as for those in general education, despite that VET provision is more expensive than general education (reflecting that practical training commonly involves special equipment, and often requires small group training to provide the necessary guidance).

Poviats are free to allocate the budget for education between schools as they see fit. Since the allocation from the national budget is generally considered insufficient, most self-governments in Poland add their own funds to cover additional expenses.

Since 2004, EU funds have been allocated to finance improvements in the quality of VET. Structural funds (from the European Social Fund and the European Regional Development Fund) are managed both nationally and regionally. At the national level, funds are used mostly for supporting structural reforms of the education system, while at the regional level funds tend to be directed toward supporting individual schools. One of the current priorities of EU Funds is to support VET, including through strengthening the cooperation between schools and enterprises, and WBL.

There is no training levy or other financing system in place to ensure private sector contributions to the funding of technical education. This is contrary to the situation in basic vocational education, where employer contributions finance costs associated with apprenticeships (box 2.2).

WORK-BASED LEARNING IN VET

Practical vocational training in VET—regulations and practice

Beyond the apprenticeship scheme in basic vocational education, VET programs in Poland hardly require students to spend any time in firms. The provision of formal VET in Poland includes three main parts: general education subjects, theoretical vocational training and practical vocational training. Apprentices participating in the juvenile worker scheme in basic vocational education tend to spend the majority of the time with their employers (box 2.2). However, basic vocational education students who do not participate in this scheme, as well as students of technical schools, are not required to spend significant time in firms. For these students (comprising around 85 percent of students enrolled in formal VET), both general education and theoretical vocational training are mainly provided by and in VET Schools. As part of practical vocational training, students in both vocational and technical schools are required to devote a part of their time to "practical activities" (*zajęcia praktyczne*). With the objective to learn the professional skills needed to commence work in a given profession, practical activities take up 38 percent of the learning program of basic vocational students, and 18 percent of those in technical education. Practical activities can take place in firms, but also in school workshops, CPTs, and CCTs. In addition to practical activities, students in technical education (but not those in vocational schools) are required to do a "traineeship" (*praktyki zawodowe*), which is aimed at applying knowledge and mastering professional skills in real working conditions. It is assumed that students participating in a traineeship have already acquired professional skills (through practical activities), and will apply them in real working conditions during the apprenticeship. The minimum required duration of traineeships depends per occupation,

BOX 2.2

Apprenticeships in basic vocational education

Well over half of students in basic vocational education are 'juvenile workers', who participate in an apprenticeship scheme. The scheme is targeted at youth from 16 to 18 years of age. Employers offering apprenticeships tend to be mainly small and medium sized enterprises specializing in crafts. Under the juvenile worker scheme, the employer is primarily responsible for both the practical and the theoretical vocational education of students, and schools provide mostly general education. Employers can also revert to basic vocational schools and other entities (such as the Centers for Education and Improvement) for the provision of theoretical vocational education that cannot be provided at the premises.

The juvenile worker scheme has several distinct features compared to the alternative of school-managed basic vocational education, as well as to technical education which is exclusively managed by schools:

- The apprenticeship arrangement is concluded through a contract between the employer and the juvenile worker.

- Juvenile workers spend approximately three days a week at the premises of the employers, and the remainder in schools.
- Juvenile workers are guaranteed a remuneration corresponding to 4–6 percent of the average wage (equivalent to approximately €40 per month in the first year of training, up to circa €60 in the third year).
- Employers offering apprenticeships receive compensation from the national Labor Fund, which is financed through employers' contributions. The amount of compensation is equivalent to the remuneration that employers are required to pay the apprentices. In addition, employers receive approximately €2,000 provided that the juvenile worker passes the vocational qualification exam.

While there appears to be a downward trend in the number of juvenile workers (in the school year 2015/16, there were 101,286 apprentices), their share among basic vocational education students has increased over the past decade, reaching 56.6 percent in the school year 2015/16 (Central Statistics Office, see figure B2.2.1).

FIGURE B2.2.1

Juvenile workers

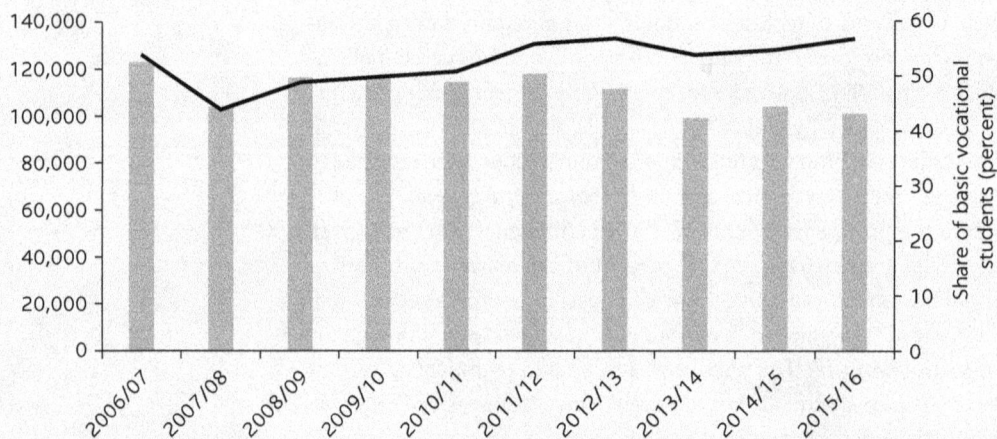

Source: Eurydice 2014.

but can be as little as four weeks over the course of the 4-year training program (the minimum requirement is never more than 12 weeks).

Depending on the interpretation of regulations, neither vocational nor technical students are required to carry out any of their training in firms at all. As for practical activities, current regulations do not prioritize any possible location for these activities over the other, and there is no formal requirement that any of the practical activities take place with employers. For traineeships for technical education students, the wording of the regulatory requirement is ambiguous: whereas some stakeholders assume that "real working conditions" refers explicitly to in-firm training, others assume that this can also refer to environments such as school workshops which aim to simulate the work floor. Applying the latter interpretation, and recalling that regulations do not require any of the practical activities to take place in firms, this implies that no in-firm learning experiences are required for VET students (with the exception of juvenile workers). Table 2.2 summarizes the key dimensions of practical activities and traineeships, for both basic vocational and technical education.

Since 2015, Poland's regulatory system for VET recognizes the possibility of "dual training," but the take-up of this option appears low. The Polish definition of dual VET does not, like in some other countries, refer to a system where

TABLE 2.2 Characteristics of two types of practical vocational training schemes in formal VET

DIMENSION	PRACTICAL ACTIVITIES	TRAINEESHIPS
School type	Basic vocational school Upper secondary technical school	Only upper secondary technical school
Location of training	School workshops Centers for Practical Training Centers for Continuing Training Employers' premises *(None of these options is prioritized in legislation)*	Regulations prescribe traineeships to take place "in real working conditions." However, the term is ambiguous, and sometimes considered to mean "in firms," and at other times to include work simulation environments such as "school workshops organized in a similar way as a work floor"
Duration of training	970 school hours in basic vocational school 735 hours in upper secondary technical school	From 4 to 12 weeks minimum, depending on the occupation (the minimal scope is defined in the core curriculum). If the scope exceeds 4 weeks, the rest of the time is taken from time devoted to practical activities
Timing of training	The training is organized during the school year and integrated into weekly schedule	The training can be organized throughout the year, including summer holidays
Contractual arrangements	For juvenile workers, training is based on a contract between the juvenile worker and the employer (mainly small and medium craft enterprises). For other students, if the training is not provided by the VET school, it is based on a contract between the school and the training provider (e.g., CPT, firm, etc.)	If the traineeship is not provided by the VET school, it is based on a contract between the school and the traineeship provider (e.g., CPT, firm, etc.)
Remuneration for students	Guaranteed only for juvenile workers (ca. 40€ a month in the first year of training, up to ca. 60€ in the third year) For other students, only if employer is willing to pay	Only if employer is willing to pay

Sources: Based on Eurydice 2014, regulatory review, and stakeholder consultations.

in-firm learning features at least as prominently as school-based training in the overall VET program. Rather, in Poland, dual training is considered to be applied when a minimum share of the required hours for practical vocational training take place in firms. For basic vocational education, the requirement is rather substantial, since all hours that are required to be spent on practical activities (970 school hours, or 38 percent of the VET program) need to be spent in-firm under the dual approach. In technical education, not more than 30 percent of the hours reserved for practical activities needs to be spent in-firm. This implies that dual VET is considered to be applied in technical education as soon as a student spends more than around 5.5 percent of the total duration of the VET program in firms (i.e., 220 school hours during the four-year training period). While no data on the incidence of dual training was available to the authors of this book it appears that its application is not widespread. The reason for the low uptake is likely the voluntary nature of this approach, combined with the absence of support mechanisms or tools to facilitate or incentivize dual training. Essentially, the extent of in-firm learning that is currently defined as "dual training" was already possible before the term was formally introduced in 2015, so it is not surprising that without any further measures to promote it, the impact may have been limited.

Less than five percent of technical education students in the region carry out practical activities in firms. In Poland as a whole, only 7.7 percent of technical education students carry out practical activities with employers (including a small share of students who carry out these activities on farms). In Świętokrzyskie, this share is still lower, at 4.3 percent (figure 2.2). The incidence of firm-based practical activities in technical education is substantially lower than in basic vocational schools, where the share of students who carry out at least part of their practical activities in firms is 66.2 percent nationwide, and 58.2 percent in Świętokrzyskie.[8]

Even traineeships, which are required to take place in firms, are sometimes carried out in schools and CPTs. Of all technical students in Świętokrzyskie,

FIGURE 2.2

Location of practical activities in technical education (share of students, 2016)

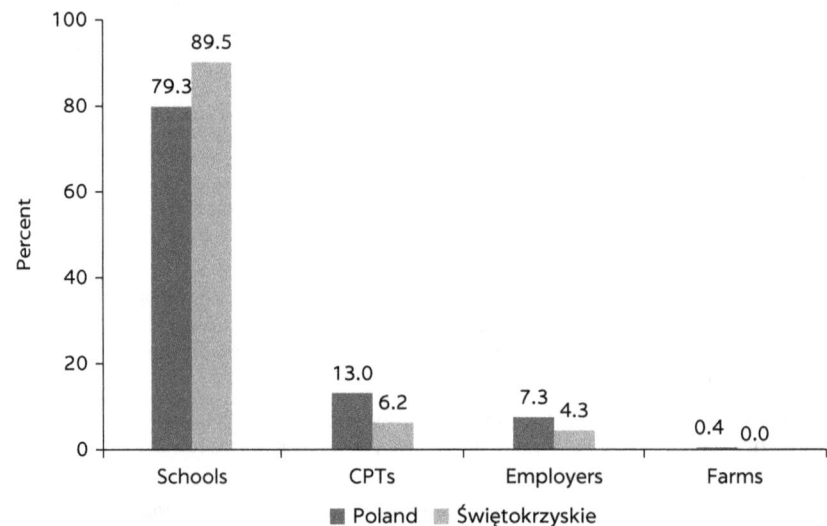

Source: Education Information System (data received from the MoNE in September 2016).

FIGURE 2.3

Location of traineeships in technical education (share of students, 2016)

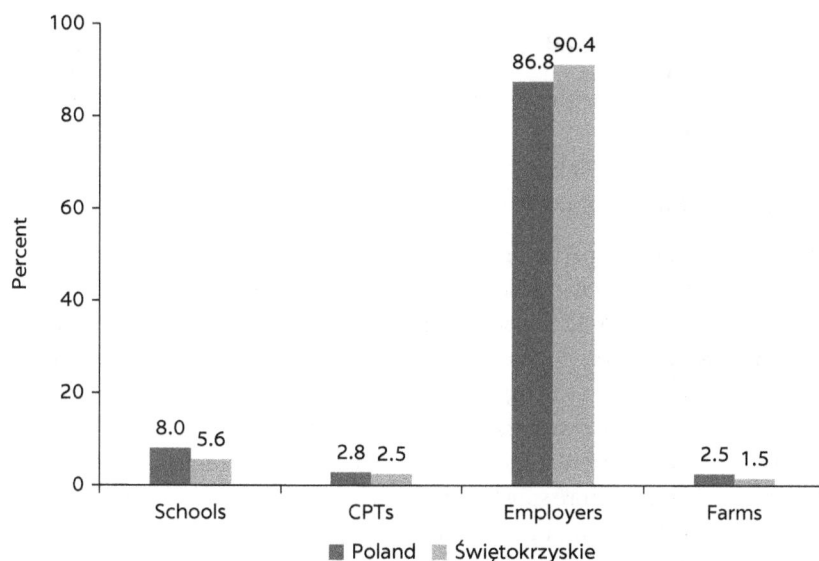

Source: Education Information System (data received from the MoNE in September 2016).

91.9 percent carry out their traineeship with employers (including on farms). While this is higher than the national average of 89.3 percent, it implies that around 8 percent of students in the region do not meet the requirement that traineeships should be carried out with employers (figure 2.3).

In addition to organizing practical vocational training in firms, other modes of school-firm collaboration exist in Poland, such as "patronage classes." Based on a contract between a VET school and a firm (and sometimes also other institutions), patronage classes are established in a particular occupation and aimed at better adapting learning outcomes to enterprise or sector skill demand. The training tends to be provided by enterprise staff, often on the firm's premises. They may involve additional admission procedures, extra-curricular activities and examinations, and sometimes include a job guarantee for students after graduation. Patronage classes exist mostly for students of basic vocational education, although they also exist for students of technical schools. In Świętokrzyskie, for example, the steelworks firm Celsa organizes patronage classes for students of mechatronics in technical schools.

School-firm arrangements in work-based learning

Key arrangements to organize and implement WBL are included in a contract between the employer and the VET school. The exception to this are the arrangements for juvenile workers which, as indicated above, are arranged through a contract between the firm and the student. Firm-school contracts define the responsibilities of both parties. In principle, the school is responsible for:

- supervising the curriculum implementation
- approving the practical training instructor proposed by the employer, or designating a practical training teacher from among the teaching staff of the school

- providing students with accident insurance and reimbursement of travel/accommodation costs (the latter in case the practical vocational training takes place in a remote locations).

The employer, on the other hand, is responsible for:

- providing students with adequately equipped training posts, working clothes, and alimentation
- designating the workplace practical training instructor
- supervising the course of workplace practical training.

By law, employers participating in WBL are entitled to receive a financial compensation; however, in practice this compensation appears rarely received. Poviat authorities should finance the employers from the education allocation that they receive from the national budget (as per the amounts in table 2.3 below). However, due to budget constraints, consultations in Świętokrzyskie highlighted that these transfers tend not to be made.

The situation is different for employers participating in the juvenile worker scheme, who receive more substantial financial support from a different source. Employers participating in the juvenile worker scheme are paid from the national Labor Fund, which is financed through employers' contributions. Employers are obliged to pay apprentices a small salary (4–6 percent of the average salary, equivalent to circa €40–60, for which they receive full compensation from the Labor Fund. In addition, they are entitled to a subsidy of circa €2,000, once the juvenile worker passes the vocational qualification exam.

An important element of arrangements between school and employer relates to the designation of the person who is responsible for guiding and supervising the student during in-firm practical activities. This can be either a teacher from the VET school ("practical training teacher") or an employee of the firm ("practical training instructor"). Firm employees cannot be practical training instructors unless they either have a teacher's qualification (for full-time instructors) or have successfully completed an 80-hours pedagogical course combined with occupational qualifications (for instructors for whom student supervision is an additional duty). These requirements are quite onerous and likely create disincentives for employers to use their own staff as instructors. The above requirements only apply in the case of "practical activities"; for firm staff who supervise of students carrying out traineeships in firms, no particular requirements exist.

TABLE 2.3 **Reimbursement for employers in work-based learning arrangements**

PURPOSE OF REIMBURSEMENT	SIZE OF REIMBURSEMENT
Practical training instructor's salary (in case training is his or her main duty)	Up to teacher's minimal salary (ca. 360€)
Practical training instructor's training supplement (in case training is his or her additional duty)	No less than 10 percent of average salary (ca. 100€)
Work clothes and shoes for students	Up to 20 percent of average salary (ca. 200€)

NOTES

1. The juvenile worker scheme is further described in the section on Work-Based Learning in VET of this chapter.
2. Enrolment in 2015/16 was as follows: 518,862 students in technical schools; 501,240 students in general secondary education; 178,809 students in basic vocational education; and 10,784 students in special needs education.
3. Regulation of the Minister of National Education of 23 December 2011 on the classification of occupations for vocational education (Journal of Laws 2012 item 7 with subsequent amendments).
4. The development of the PQF is managed by the Polish Education Research Institute under the auspices of the Ministry of National Education. It is described as "top-down and research driven", potentially posing some challenges to ensure commitment and ownership to the process beyond the public sector (CEDEFOP 2015)
5. As technical education results in the *matura* exam in addition to a vocational qualification, graduates can access post-secondary and tertiary education. The share of young VET graduates in further education and training in Poland was 38.4 percent in 2010, which is above the EU average of 30.7 percent (CEDEFOP 2017). While further education might discourage employers from providing work placements (as students may not be available for employment immediately after graduation), this was not identified as a constraint by employers during consultations.
6. There are 16 regions in Poland, each with a population of between 1 and 5 million persons. The Świętokrzyskie region, which is the focus of this book has approximately 1.3 million inhabitants.
7. The Świętokrzyskie region contains fourteen *poviats* with populations ranging from circa 34,000 to 209,000 inhabitants. In addition to regions and *poviats* a third level of local government are gmina.
8. For basic vocational students who do not participate in the apprenticeship scheme, the share is circa 20 percent nationwide.

REFERENCES

CEDEFOP. 2015. *Publication Analysis and Overview of NQF Developments in European Countries. Annual Report 2014. Poland.* http://www.cedefop.europa.eu/en/publications-and-resources/country-reports/poland-european-inventory-nqf-2014.

——. 2017. "On the Way to 2020: Data for Vocational Education and Training Policies. Country Statistical Overviews—2016 Update." Cedefop Research Paper 61. Publications Office, Luxembourg.

Central Statistical Office. 2016. *Education in 2015/2016 School Year.* Warsaw: Central Statistical Office.

Eurydice. 2014. *The System of Education in Poland.* Polish Eurydice Unit and Foundation for the Development of the Education System. Warsaw, Poland. http://www.fss.org.pl/sites/fss.org.pl/files/the-system_2014_www_0.pdf

3 Key Dimensions for Improved Work-Based Learning in Technical Education in Świętokrzyskie

Weaknesses in the quality and relevance of VET are considered to constrain the growth potential of Poland's Świętokrzyskie region, and these challenges are assumed to result among others from the absence of strong work-based learning elements in technical education. The regulatory framework allows a substantial share of training to take place in firms, but nevertheless the incidence, duration, and quality or WBL in technical education in Świętokrzyskie, as in Poland as a whole, is limited.

This chapter presents the analytical framework identifying the key dimensions that determine the incidence, duration, and quality of WBL. This framework is subsequently applied to assess and describe the main challenges to effective WBL implementation in technical education in Świętokrzyskie. For each of the challenges, examples are provided on how they are addressed in (mostly European) countries outside of Poland.

SUMMARY: KEY DIMENSIONS THAT DETERMINE EFFECTIVE WORK-BASED LEARNING

A general analytical framework for effective WBL

In 2015, the European Commission (EC) published guidance on the main aspects that determine the effective delivery of WBL (European Commission 2015). The "20 guiding principles" identified in this book (summarized in box 3.1) are clustered in four categories, relating to mechanisms for governance and engagement of social partners; support for companies; the attractiveness of WBL and career guidance for students; and quality assurance (QA) in WBL.

BOX 3.1

Twenty guiding principles for effective WBL

A. National Governance and Social Partners' Engagement

1. A clear and consistent legal framework which enables all work-based learning (WBL) partners to act effectively and guarantee mutual rights and responsibilities

2. A structured, continuous dialogue with a transparent method of coordination and decision making between all WBL partners

3. Strong ownership and implementation of social partners, supported through capacity building

4. Systematic and effective cooperation between VET schools or training centers and companies

5. All WBL partners (companies, VET providers, learners) share costs and benefits.

B. Support for companies, in particular for small and medium enterprises (SMEs), which participate in WBL

6. Support measures are in place that make WBL more attractive and accessible, especially for SMEs

7. Achieving the right balance between skill needs of firms and learning needs of students

8. Particular attention is paid to supporting firms without experience in WBL provision

9. Particular attention is paid to supporting firms offering WBL to disadvantaged learners

10. Companies are motivated and supported to assign qualified trainers and tutors

C. Attractiveness of WBL and career guidance

11. Pathways between VET and other education and career pathways exist

12. The image of VET and WBL are improved by promoting excellence

13. Sound career guidance is provided to ensure young people make well-founded choices

14. The attractiveness of WBL by raising the quality of VET teachers

15. The attractiveness of VET and WBL is promoted through a broad range of awareness-raising activities.

D. Quality Assurance in WBL

16. A clear framework for quality assurance exists at the system, provider, and company levels, with systematic feedback

17. Training provision is responsive to changing skill needs in companies and society

18. Mutual trust and respect between WBL partners is fostered through regular cooperation

19. The assessment of learning outcomes is fair, valid, and authentic

20. In-firm trainers can access continuous professional development and have adequate working conditions.

Source: European Commission 2015.

Six priority dimensions to strengthen WBL implementation in Świętokrzyskie

The above-described "20 principles," combined with a review of relevant policy documentation and intensive stakeholder consultations, were used as a basis to identify the priority dimensions that need to be addressed to strengthen WBL implementation in technical education in Świętokrzyskie. Key considerations that informed the identification of the key priorities in the region related to the following:

- *Prioritizing among the 20 principles:* The current low incidence and duration of WBL is due to weaknesses in all of the clusters and dimensions that are identified in the EC's analytical framework. The criteria applied to prioritize among the various dimensions included:

BOX 3.2

Six priority dimensions for strengthening work-based learning in technical education Świętokrzyskie

1. An appropriate governance and financing framework
2. Effective mechanisms for stakeholder consultation and coordination
3. Adequate incentives and capacity of VET providers
4. Adequate incentives and capacity of firms
5. Quality assurance (QA) mechanisms for work-based learning (WBL)
6. A facilitating role for centers for practical training (CPT).

- – A focus on dimensions that are *directly and exclusively related to WBL*, such as the legal framework for WBL provision and support to firms for WBL implementation[1]
- – A focus on dimensions that are *structurally impeding overall WBL implementation* (rather than specifically targeting hard-to-reach stakeholders such as small and medium sized firms)

- *Adding relevant priorities:* an important impediment to WBL implementation in Świętokrzyskie that was absent from the original "20 principles" relates to weak incentives and capacity of both VET providers and CPTs. This aspect has thus been added as a key priority for the region.

The resulting dimensions that were determined to be key priorities in Świętokrzyskie are the following (box 3.2):

The requirements for each of these dimensions to contribute appropriately to effective WBL implementation are summarized below. Combined, the six dimensions result in a strong focus on facilitating key stakeholders through providing them with the appropriate incentives and capacity to effectively implement WBL.

Six priority dimensions for WBL implementation in technical education in Świętokrzyskie

1. **An appropriate governance and financing framework**
   - The regulatory framework guiding WBL is clear and prescribes sufficiently high minimum criteria for the incidence and duration of WBL, while providing adequate flexibility to providers and firms to implement context-appropriate solutions
   - Monitoring, accountability and financing mechanisms facilitate the effective implementation of WBL.
2. **Effective mechanisms for stakeholder consultation and coordination**
   - Regional and/or local stakeholder platforms with a broad range of stakeholders provide strategic directions and identify and address key constraints to WBL implementation, with a focus on strengthening collaboration between VET provides and enterprises
   - Effective support mechanisms assist individual stakeholders in WBL implementation (particularly to strengthen incentives and capacity of VET providers and schools, see points 3 and 4 below).

3. **Adequate incentives and capacity of VET providers**
   - VET providers have sufficient incentives to transition from school-based VET provision to an increasingly WBL-based VET system
   - VET providers have the technical and financial capacity to increase the incidence, duration, and quality of WBL.
4. **Adequate incentives and capacity of firms**
   - Firms are aware of the direct and longer term benefits of WBL provision
   - Firms are aware of the regulations concerning WBL provision
   - Firms have the capacity to engage in WBL in a manner that maximizes direct firm benefits, and that minimizes the costs associated with WBL provision
   - Firms receive appropriate financial incentives and technical assistance to facilitate the provision of high quality WBL.
5. **Quality assurance mechanisms for WBL**
   - The achievement of appropriate learning outcomes is assured through clear and effective QA mechanisms, within which the division of responsibilities between VET providers, firms, and students is clearly delineated.
6. **A facilitating role for Centers for Practical Training**
   - Work-environment simulating training provided in CPT is responsive to skill demand, and facilitates (rather than competes with) WBL provided in firms.

   The next sections in this chapter will elaborate on the strengths and, particularly, the challenges of each dimension within the Świętokrzyskie context (which in some cases applies to the overall Polish context). The key challenges for Świętokrzyskie related to each dimension are summarized in table 3.1 below. Each section will also provide international examples on how these

TABLE 3.1 **Key dimensions and challenges in Świętokrzyskie for strengthening WBL in technical education**

PRIORITY DIMENSION	KEY CHALLENGES
1. **Appropriate governance and financing framework**	• Low minimum requirements for the duration of in-firm learning • Elements of regulations related to WBL are ambiguous • Accountability mechanisms do not explicitly promote WBL • Financing mechanisms are not effective in providing incentives for WBL • Policy measures and intentions are not accompanied by implementation support mechanisms • The regulatory environment is unstable and not strongly reinforced by measures that facilitate its implementation
2. **Effective mechanisms for stakeholder consultation and coordination**	• A structural mechanism for effective coordination and collaboration among a wider range of stakeholders remains to emerge (existing coordination and collaboration is mostly limited to partnerships between an individual VET provider and enterprise); • Stakeholders lack incentives, capacity, and financing to engage in WBL • No "WBL champion" has yet emerged as a strong prime mover and promoter of effective consultation and collaboration mechanisms.
3. **Adequate incentives and capacity of VET providers**	• VET providers have insufficient organizational and technical capacity, tools, and human resources to engage in effective WBL implementation • VET providers have concerns about the quality of training that can, at this stage, be provided through WBL • Incentives exist to provide practical training in CPTs, rather than in firms • Reform reluctance is exacerbated by concerns about the impact of increased WBL on the demand for teaching staff and teachers' skills

continued

TABLE 3.1, *continued*

PRIORITY DIMENSION	KEY CHALLENGES
4. **Adequate incentives and capacity of firms**	• Costs associated with engaging in WBL tend to be high, and actual and perceived benefits tend to be low • Costs are relatively high since firms tend to lack the capacity and tools to engage in WBL in an effective manner • Functional mechanisms to provide financial compensation to firms are largely absent • Firms do not reap direct benefits from WBL, since students do not tend to contribute to production processes • Employers appear to not take into account all potential medium and longer term benefits of WBL • WBL engagement tends to be insufficiently marketed to have a marked impact on a firm's image • Enterprises do not necessarily consider VET providers as sound partners
5. **Quality assurance mechanisms for WBL**	• The current QA system for VET does not yet incorporate key recognized good practices to ensure demand-responsiveness of training provision, and is not specifically geared toward assuring the quality of WBL provision • No regulations or clear guidance is made available to firms and schools to guide them in carrying out sound quality assurance of WBL
6. **A facilitating role for CPTs**	• The current operating model of CPTs discourages, rather than facilitates, a stronger focus on WBL, since CPTs "compete with" or "crowd-out" in-firm training provision • Mechanisms to ensure the relevance and demand-responsiveness of training provision in CPTs tend to be weak

Source: World Bank
Note: WBL = work-based learning; VET = Vocational education and training; CPT = Center for Practical Training; QA = Quality assurance.

challenges can be addressed and, based on these, provide possible applications in Świętokrzyskie or, more broadly, within Poland. Furthermore, each section includes a summary of how the expected forthcoming WBL pilot project in Świętokrzyskie will address the dimension—a more comprehensive summary of the pilot project can also be found in chapter 4 of this book.

PRIORITY DIMENSION 1: AN APPROPRIATE GOVERNANCE AND FINANCING FRAMEWORK FOR WBL

Areas for improvement

Poland's regulations related to WBL offer the opportunity to provide a large share of training through WBL. Requirements pertaining to the scope of in-firm training provision are flexible, which offer VET providers and firms the opportunity to adapt the duration and approach of WBL to their needs and possibilities.

However, the regulatory and governance system does not appear to provide sufficient incentives to VET providers and firms to engage in WBL beyond the very limited scope that is the current practice among most stakeholders. In particular:

• **There are no minimum requirements for the duration of WBL.** While training providers have the option to implement the "dual system," which requires a minimum of 30 percent of practical learning (i.e., 220 school hours in 4-year cycle) to take place in firms, the majority of VET providers do not exercise this option. Under the "non-dual" approach, there is no minimum number of hours that students are required to spend in firms.

- **Regulations related to WBL are at times ambiguous and unclear.** This relates, for example, to the different objectives and approaches of "practical activities" and "traineeships," and the extent to which each of these should be provided in firms. The interpretation of these elements of the regulations appear to vary among stakeholders.

- **Accountability mechanisms do not explicitly promote WBL.** VET providers and their governing bodies do not tend to be held accountable for the incidence and quality of WBL. VET provider performance tends to be largely assessed based on students' final exam results; possible measures to assess employment outcomes of VET graduates through, for example, graduate tracer studies, are not or rarely applied. As the content and approach to examinations are not necessarily well-geared toward measuring the acquisition of practical and market-relevant skills that can be acquired through WBL, this does not provide incentives to providers to increase the WBL-elements in training provision.

- **Financing mechanisms do not take into account the relatively high costs associated with VET, nor do they provide incentives for WBL provision.** Financial allocations from the national budget for VET do not take into account the higher costs associated with the provision of VET compared to general education, implying that the onus of ensuring sufficient budget for VET provision is with local governments, which often face financial constraints. This appears to result, for example, in situations where firms that participate in WBL do not receive the financial compensation to which they are entitled according to the regulations, and VET providers are unable to cover the costs of transitioning to WBL-focused training provision. Like the regulatory system, the financing mechanism does not provide explicit incentives for stronger WBL provision, for example, through the incorporation of performance-based budgeting elements.

- **The regulatory environment is unstable and not strongly reinforced by measures that facilitate its implementation.** Regulatory changes are relatively frequent, causing uncertainty among practitioners about the future policy environment. For example, after rather substantial TVET reforms were initiated in 2012, further significant changes are expected to take effect from the school year 2017/2018 (see box 2.1 in "VET in the Poland's Education System" section). Moreover, policy reforms and intentions are not always strongly supported by measures to facilitate their implementation. An example of this is the introduction of the option to implement "dual VET," which was introduced in 2015, which appears to have amounted to the introduction of a new term in the regulations, without associated support or incentive mechanisms for practitioners to increase the incidence and duration of in-firm learning.

PRIORITY DIMENSION 2: EFFECTIVE MECHANISMS FOR STAKEHOLDER CONSULTATION AND COORDINATION

Coordination and collaboration among a relatively wide range of stakeholders is essential to ensure optimal WBL provision. In addition to individual firms, VET providers, and CPTs, such coordination and collaboration mechanisms ideally also include local and regional governments and stakeholders such as enterprise representatives (e.g., regional or sectoral employers' associations), labor unions, and labor market institutions that monitor employment trends and skill demand (in the case of Poland, these would be the regional labor market councils).

Stakeholder coordination and collaboration can focus on various activities, ranging from strategic planning to supporting individual stakeholders in implementing WBL. For example, activities can include:

- Targeting efforts to strengthen WBL to those occupations for which there are strong current and expected future labor market needs, and/or for which WBL is considered especially useful to ensure the acquisition of essential skills by VET students
- Determining procedures and processes for effective WBL implementation, including related to cost-sharing, quality assurance arrangements, and capacity building
- Knowledge sharing to disseminate and allow replication of best practices for WBL provision and
- Identifying and addressing bottlenecks to WBL implementation that occur at the regional, local, or individual stakeholder level.

Areas for improvement

Coordination and collaboration on WBL in Świętokrzyskie takes place, but is mostly limited to some partnerships between individual VET providers and enterprises. Provider-firm collaboration takes the form of, for example, patronage classes or student visits to enterprises. Incentives for collaboration between VET providers appear to be impeded by "competition" between providers in different *poviats* (or even in the same poviat), resulting from *poviats* and schools operating under tight financial constraints in a system where financing is directly related to number of students.

A structural mechanism for effective coordination and collaboration among a wider range of stakeholders remains to emerge, and there is currently no structure in place that supports individual stakeholders in WBL implementation. Regional or local VET strategies have not been developed,[2] and effective multi-stakeholder fora engaging in strengthening VET provision in general, and WBL implementation in particular, are absent. While structures with a potential mandate to promote firm-school collaboration exist, such as the VET cluster

FIGURE 3.1

Stakeholders in the VET system in Świętokrzyskie

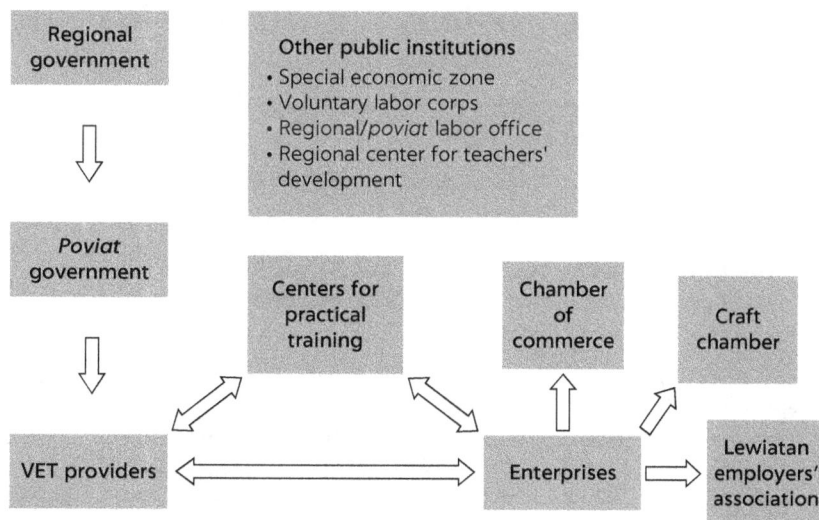

Source: World Bank.

managed by the Świętokrzyskie Special Economic Zone (SEZ), these are currently not carrying out such tasks.

Various existing entities can, in theory, play a role in facilitating coordination and collaboration. Figure 3.1 below shows various stakeholders that could be engaged in WBL-related coordination and collaboration. In addition to the regional and local governments, VET providers, enterprises, and CPTs, there are various other entities that could potentially lead or participate in WBL-coordination structures. These include the management of the Świętokrzyskie Special Economic Zone (SEZ); the Voluntary Labor Corps (VLC)—which aims to socially and professionally activate excluded youth and plays a strong role in arranging apprenticeships in basic vocational education; regional and local-level labor offices; the Świętokrzyskie Chamber of Commerce; and the Regional Center for Teachers' Development (RCTD). Some of these institutions have a formal mandate or have made initial efforts to engage in WBL coordination, but their capacity is weak. The SEZ is intended to play a role in strengthening linkages between the education system and the private sector. While it has established a "regional cluster for VET" that is to serve as a consultation body for demand-responsive VET provision, stakeholders tend to perceive it as ineffective.[3] Similarly, while labor offices are expected to provide labor market information that could be used to improve the responsiveness of education and training to market demand, the regional and local offices in Świętokrzyskie are not yet effectively providing these services. No strong efforts to coordinate WBL have been made by the regional Chamber of Commerce or any other body that represents groups of enterprises, potentially due to a lack of capacity combined with different priorities.

Introducing strong elements of WBL in a largely school-based VET system comprises a strong deviation from "doing business as usual" for all stakeholders involved. Such a transition is unlikely to materialize unless there is a strong push from at least one key actor to bring various stakeholders together. Absent strong incentives that are provided from the national level, one or more regional-level champions would need to emerge to lead these efforts. To date, none of the potential actors has shown to be both willing and able to take on this role effectively. This appears to be due to a combination of factors related to incentives (since no stakeholder appears to consider strengthening WBL coordination as among their key objectives, or is held accountable for WBL coordination); capacity (since key stakeholders lack the experience and knowledge for effective WBL coordination), and financing (since even stakeholders with mandates to strengthen WBL appear not to allocate financing to this task).

International practices

Stakeholder collaboration and coordination mechanisms can be organized in different ways, taking into account several dimensions:

- *Territorial*: at national, regional, local, and school level. In many countries, bodies operating on different levels coexist, and different levels complement each other.
- *Sectorial*: some mechanisms can cover the whole territory, while others target specific sectors or occupations, focusing on the relevance and accuracy of curricula and WBL practices for a select number of qualifications.
- *Organizational*: leadership and management of collaboration mechanisms can be the responsibility of public institutions (e.g., VET agencies), social partners (such as chambers of commerce, employers' associations, or labor unions), or collective bodies (such as skills councils).

Examples of collaboration mechanisms that promote coordination and/or support include the Apprenticeship Offices in Austria, and the Local Training Committees in Denmark. The Austrian Apprenticeship Offices are located in the regional Economic Chambers, and are the main contact point for companies for questions related to apprenticeships (box 3.3). The Danish Local Training Committees comprise representatives of actors with a stake in demand-responsive VET provision, and among others work to ensure suitable WBL placements for students (box 3.4).

BOX 3.3

Austria—apprenticeship offices

The apprenticeship system in Austria is managed on the regional level by Apprenticeship Offices (AO). There are nine offices, one in each region. They are located in the regional economic chambers. They are the main contact point for companies and must in principle take care of all questions concerning apprenticeship, and provide consultation and advice. They are supported in this by the apprenticeship and youth protection offices of the regional chambers of labor.

In particular, AO are responsible for the following areas of the apprenticeship system:

- Accreditation of training companies—AO examine the training companies' suitability to provide apprenticeship training in subject specific and staff-related respects. They collaborate in this with representatives of the regional chambers of labor

- Handling of apprenticeship contracts
- Legal advice to the stakeholders of the apprenticeships system
- Coordination of apprenticeship-leave examinations—a heads of AO appoint the chairpersons of the apprenticeship-leave examination boards on the basis of a proposal to be obtained from the Regional Advisory Board on Apprenticeship
- Subsidies for training companies
- Career guidance
- Support of talented apprentices
- Seeking out and involving new companies in the apprenticeship system—AO have "training companies' scouts" who inform potential training companies about the possibilities of training, motivate the companies to offer training places and provide advisory support.

Sources: Federal Ministry of Economy, Family and Youth 2014; ReferNet 2014a.

BOX 3.4

Denmark—local training committees

In Denmark, each VET school is attached to at least one (depending on the occupations taught) local training committee to assist with its VET provision. The training committees consist of representatives of local employers and employees, appointed by national trade committees, as well as representatives of staff, management and students appointed by college. Training committees work closely alongside colleges in developing the curriculum to make sure that the VET programs are adapted to specific skills needs. Training committees also work towards the development of cooperation with local trade and industry and help to ensure enough suitable local training placements.

Local training committees also assist and advise national trade committees in approving local enterprises as qualified training establishments and in mediating conflicts between apprentices and enterprises.

Sources: Cedefop 2012; ReferNet 2014b.

Applications for Świętokrzyskie

A "critical mass" of key stakeholders in the region appears to have increased their interest in WBL implementation, as a result of the recent intensive engagement under the Catching-Up Regions initiative. These stakeholders include VET providers and enterprises, as well as the regional and several local governments. While stakeholder capacity to implement WBL is still rather low, this implies that there appear to be stakeholders that would be willing to actively engage in coordination and collaboration activities.

An effective entity that will lead WBL coordination in Świętokrzyskie is unlikely to emerge unless constraints related to incentives, capacity, and financing are addressed simultaneously. International practices highlight that strong institutional structures to support individual VET providers and firms are essential to ensure WBL implementation. This is also assumed to be the case in Świętokrzyskie. However, while some first steps have been made to pave the way for stakeholder coordination—such as the establishment of the SEZ's regional cluster for VET—there are no signs that either of these entities will be taking further steps to concretely carry out WBL coordination activities.

The pilot project on Implementation of Work-Based Learning in Świętokrzyskie is expected to lay the groundworks for future structural collaboration mechanisms. The project, which is financed by European Social Fund (ESF) under Operational Programme Knowledge Education Development (OP KED), will initiate collaboration and coordination between participating VET providers and enterprises, associated local governments, and the regional government, as part of the initiative which entails the piloting of various approaches to WBL implementation across the region. In addition to facilitating concrete stakeholder collaboration during implementation, the project is also expected to generate lessons which can be used to scale-up the initiative, including on the approaches and entity (or entities) that is (are) most appropriate to promote structural stakeholder coordination mechanisms in the future.

PRIORITY DIMENSION 3: ADEQUATE INCENTIVES AND CAPACITY OF VET PROVIDERS

Areas for improvement

The regulatory framework offers sufficient flexibility to VET providers to incorporate substantial elements of WBL in their training offer, and most VET providers have at least some engagement with firms. Provider-firm interactions relate mostly to the provision of traineeships, which are in principle required to take place in firms. A limited number of VET providers have additional interactions with firms, such as on the provision of patronage classes by enterprises, which generally take place outside of the regular curriculum.

However, substantial constraints related to incentives and capacity hamper the provision of effective WBL, and more broadly a move away from supply-driven VET provision. To an extent, and as already highlighted above, these impediments are due to the regulatory, governance, and financing framework, which leads training providers to focus on implementing the core curriculum without strong regard for the acquisition of demand-responsive skills through WBL (see Priority Dimension 1). Other constraints relate to weaknesses in the overall VET and WBL eco-system, such as the lack of coordination and collaboration structures and of reliable labor demand data, which increase the onus for WBL implementation on individual schools (see Priority Dimension 2). Beyond these obstacles, additional school-specific constraints include a combination of further disincentives, and insufficient technical capacity and human resources, as follows:

- **There are legitimate concerns about the quality and scope of training that can, at this stage, be provided through WBL.** Considering the scant experience with effective WBL provision, combined with the lack of quality assurance tools, schools have justifiable concerns about expanding WBL provision unless the achievement of appropriate learning outcomes through WBL can be ensured. Current concerns include, among others, a lack of tools to ensure that firms strike an appropriate balance between focusing on particular skills that are required within the enterprise compared to those defined in the curriculum; and insufficient mechanisms to assess learning outcomes acquired through WBL.

- **Schools have incentives to provide practical vocational training either themselves or through CPT, rather than in firms.** Working with CPTs is easier to arrange for schools than WBL. Moreover, consultations highlighted that VET providers may perceive pressure to work with CPTs, due to apparent concerns that a transition from CPTs to firm-based training will reduce the demand for CPT staff, and potentially also considering that nationwide ESF indicators include an indicator related to the extent to which ESF-financed equipment in CPTs is used for training provision, and

- **VET providers lack the technical capacity, tools, and human resources to engage in effective WBL implementation**. Lack of experience in effective WBL provision (including establishing effective collaboration with firms, adapting the curriculum to include WBL, measuring WBL learning outcomes, etc.), combined with the lack of practical support tools or guidance substantially complicates the implementation of WBL even for those VET providers who are keen to strengthen WBL despite the limited incentives. Moreover, while in principle schools could reallocate existing teaching staff to tasks related to WBL provision, the transition from a school-based to a more WBL-based system is at least initially expected to require additional human resources to manage this process.

- **Reform reluctance is exacerbated by concerns about the impact of increased firm-based training on the demand for teaching staff and teachers' skills.** Concerns that stronger WBL provision will result in reduced demand for teaching staff in VET schools (whether justified or not) reduces the appetite for reform. Moreover, many teachers' technical skills are considered to be outdated and their experience with real-life working environment is limited; these are constraints which will become more apparent and significant once the work and school environment become more intertwined, which may reduce incentives to engage in WBL among teaching staff, especially as long as opportunities for upgrading teachers' skills remain limited.

International practices

With the exception of documentation that focuses on preparing VET teachers, literature on promoting WBL generally devotes little attention to the need to ensure sufficient incentives and capacity of VET providers when they transition from a largely school-based system.

However, analyses carried out by the European Training Foundation (ETF) in a variety of countries which attempted such a transition, underline a few critical elements that facilitate the process.[4] The policy lessons identified by the ETF relate to incentivizing all stakeholders and promoting their effective interactions. Those particularly relevant for effectively engaging VET providers are summarized below (based on European Training Foundation 2014). The full list of policy lessons can be found in appendix B.

- **Involve all key stakeholders**, including VET providers, and ensure that they share the same vision
- **Avoid competition** between the preferred approach and other existing approaches to WBL or other forms of practical learning. Competition can occur when different schemes exist for employers, students or social partners. In the case of Poland, such competition currently exists between WBL (in-firm practical activities and traineeships) and school and CPT-based practical learning
- **Start with pilot programs**, which include strong monitoring and evaluation systems generating lessons that can be incorporated in subsequent activities
- **Invest substantial efforts in building tools** needed to support the new WBL approach, including on competency standards, curricula, skill lists for enterprises and students, and assessment tools
- **Invest substantial effort in building capacity** of the individuals who need to implement the new approach at the local level: enterprise tutors or trainers, vocational teachers, curriculum developers and social partners
- **Actively market and communicate** the new approach to all key stakeholders, at the local and regional levels in addition to the national level.

Latvia, Denmark, and Finland all include elements in their policies that aim to strengthen and maintain the capacity and incentives of VET providers to facilitate WBL. Latvia is an example of a country which is moving to increased WBL in VET from a largely school-based system, taking into account most of the best-practices as identified by the ETF (box 3.5). In Denmark, all vocational colleges employ advisors ("LOP-konsulenter") responsible for promoting cooperation between vocational colleges and companies and for facilitating WBL placements (ReferNet 2014b). Interventions aimed at teachers often relate to updating their skills in line with the skill needs in particular industries, including for example through in-work training for teachers, organized in enterprises, as is practiced in Finland (box 3.6).

Applications for Świętokrzyskie

Good practices related to stakeholder engagement and communication, producing tools and building capacity, and upgrading teacher competencies can be introduced at the regional level without the need for national-level reforms. Some WBL pilots are already taking place in Świętokrzyskie (and in other parts of Poland),

Strengthening work-based learning in Latvia

As in Poland, VET provision in Latvia is largely school-based. In 2012, Latvia initiated efforts to strengthen WBL, as part of a broader VET reform that also included network optimization, legal reforms, and stronger engagement of social partners.

Reform efforts were guided by intensive consultations, championed by the Ministry of Education, and resulting in small-scale pilot interventions that applied a bottom-up approach in terms of design. Subsequently, based on the results of the three-year pilot, the regulatory framework related to WBL was adapted to allow for a further, structural expansion of WBL provision. The implementation of WBL under the new framework commenced in 2016, and the first results are expected to materialize in the coming years.

Key elements of the implemented approach are as follow:

- A high priority given to WBL by national authorities (Ministry of Education and Science)

- A strong focus on stakeholder consultations, resulting in a shared vision and strong ownership of the reforms
- A bottom-up pilot initiative preceded and informed the adaptation of the regulatory framework
- The consultation and reform process was informed by international practices, particularly through strong cooperation with stakeholders from countries with well-established WBL mechanisms, such as Germany and Switzerland
- Extensive and focused use of EU financing (particularly from the European Social Fund) will support the implementation of the WBL reform from 2016 to 2023, and is expected to contribute to the participation of 11,000 students in WBL activities.

Finland—teachers' work placement periods

The Finnish National Board of Education (FNBE), which oversees the national educational system, provides guidelines on the development of teachers' competencies. The *Requirements for Continuing Education in Teachers' Working Life Competences* (RCE) were first published in 2003. A systemic part of teachers' professional development are the work placement periods.

According to the RCE, a work placement period must last at least two months. The education provider can define a teacher-specific schedule for the implementation of work placement periods, concerning intervals between periods (typically 3–5 years), length of the period, time schedule (e.g., one period, several shorter periods, one day per week for a longer period of time), company

arrangements (in one or many companies etc.), contents of the period.

The work placement periods can serve different goals, according to the needs of the VET provider, for example:

- Develop and update teachers' vocational skills
- Create contacts with companies for further cooperation
- Plan and organize work-based learning in collaboration with company representatives
- Train in-company trainers on how to teach students.

Work placement periods should be an integral part of VET providers' strategy and policy. The Finnish system puts much emphasis on planning and evaluation.

continued

Box 3.6, *continued*

Therefore, setting up goals for work placement periods and reporting on it are in fact as important as being in the company. (See figure B3.6.1 for an example of a planning and implementation process for a teacher's work placement period.) Work placement periods are often supervised and the final report is obligatory, serving two main purposes:

1. To describe experiences in such a form that it can easily be shared within the educational institution and with various stakeholders
2. To reflect on the teacher's own learning and development process, to make the most use of the period.

FIGURE B3.6.1

An example of planning and implementation of teacher workplace periods by an educational provider

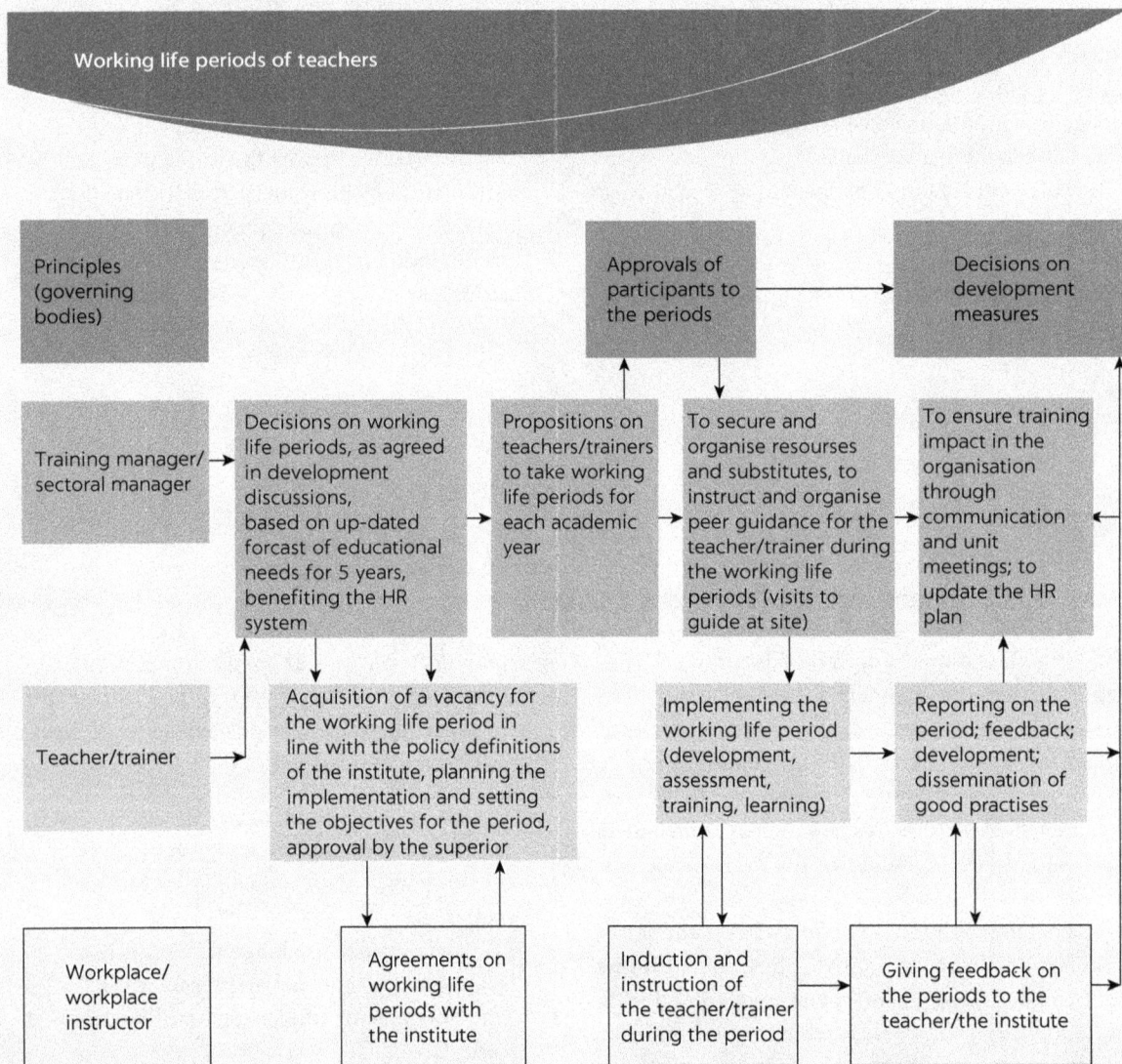

Working life periods of teachers				

Principles (governing bodies)			Approvals of participants to the periods	Decisions on development measures
Training manager/ sectoral manager	Decisions on working life periods, as agreed in development discussions, based on up-dated forcast of educational needs for 5 years, benefiting the HR system	Propositions on teachers/trainers to take working life periods for each academic year	To secure and organise resourses and substitutes, to instruct and organise peer guidance for the teacher/trainer during the working life periods (visits to guide at site)	To ensure training impact in the organisation through communication and unit meetings; to update the HR plan
Teacher/trainer	Acquisition of a vacancy for the working life period in line with the policy definitions of the institute, planning the implementation and setting the objectives for the period, approval by the superior		Implementing the working life period (development, assessment, training, learning)	Reporting on the period; feedback; development; dissemination of good practises
Workplace/ workplace instructor	Agreements on working life periods with the institute		Induction and instruction of the teacher/trainer during the period	Giving feedback on the periods to the teacher/the institute

Source: Tarja 2014.

and a worthwhile start could be to generate and disseminate their lessons learned to a broader audience. While the challenge of competing approaches and incentives for practical learning cannot be addressed at the regional level alone, as they are likely to require national-level reforms, there appear to be no unsurmountable barriers to initiating regional or local initiatives to implement the other identified good practices. What this does require, however, is a champion and a critical mass of stakeholders to manage and engage in collaboration and coordination activities (see Priority Dimension 2), as well as sufficient financing and technical capacity to develop tools, provide capacity building activities, and develop processes such as for in-firm training of teachers.

The pilot project on Implementation of Work-Based Learning in Świętokrzyskie is expected to finance and provide technical assistance to help increase capacity and incentives for VET providers in the coming years. Among others, the project aims to support a number of qualifying VET providers through providing intensive and needs-based technical assistance (related to, among others, collaborating with enterprises, adapting curricula, and developing quality assurance mechanisms); developing relevant tools for WBL implementation; and offering financing to cover the costs of additional human resources that are needed to facilitate WBL provision.

The pilot project is expected to generate lessons and further incentives for developing more sustainable and longer-term mechanisms to improve capacity and incentives of VET providers. At the level of individual schools, this may include facilitating the opportunity of school staff to allocate sufficient time to WBL implementation, for example by focusing on contacts with enterprises, adapting curricula to incorporate WBL, monitoring WBL placements, and ensuring proper teachers' training (Frisk 2014).

PRIORITY DIMENSION 4: ADEQUATE INCENTIVES AND CAPACITY OF FIRMS

It is assumed that firms' willingness to engage in WBL is mostly determined by a rational consideration of its costs and benefits. Costs include both the actual costs of providing WBL (including compensation of students who participate in WBL, expenditures on material and equipment used for training purposes without contributing to the firms' production processes, or on staff recruited to manage WBL processes) and opportunity costs (e.g., staff time, material, or equipment that is used for WBL provision rather than for contributing to production processes). Benefits, in principle, are generated in various ways: the most direct benefits are through the active contribution in production processes of students who participate in WBL, who thus basically provide relatively cheap labor to the firm. Additional benefits include reduced transaction costs for recruiting well-qualified new workers from graduated WBL students, as well as contributing to creating a larger pool of qualified labor, which reduces skills shortages and thus, expectedly, labor costs. A more immaterial benefit is that participation in WBL can result in a more positive image of an enterprise among both potential future employees and the wider public, which could increase both the willingness of workers to be employed by these firms, and of consumers to obtain the firms' products or services.

Areas for improvement

In Świętokrzyskie, firms' costs associated with engaging in WBL tend to be high, and both actual and perceived benefits tend to be low. As a result, the (actual and perceived) cost-benefit ratio of WBL participation is too high for many firms to be willing to engage in WBL. In particular:

- **Costs are high, since firms tend to lack the capacity and tools to engage in WBL in an efficient manner.** For example, firms have little experience in achieving an appropriate balance between meeting students' learning needs as prescribed by the curriculum, and ensuring that students add value to the production process. A lack of expertise in teaching approaches and pedagogical skills of company staff also implies that firm employees tend to spend more time than needed teaching and overseeing WBL-students, which increases the opportunity costs of WBL provision. The lack of coordination and support mechanisms to build capacity or promote firm-school engagement implies that firms have very limited means to reduce such costs. For example, while legislation prescribes that in-firm instructors should undergo a pedagogical course, the quality of such courses is unclear

- **Due among others to local authorities' financial constraints, no functional mechanisms exist to compensate firms** for direct and/or opportunity costs associated with WBL provision. For example, as indicated earlier, while firms are entitled to reimbursement for practical training instructor's pay and for working clothing for students, in practice firms are discouraged from claiming this compensation due to financial constraints of the local authorities

- **Direct benefits tend to be non-existent, since students do not tend to contribute to production processes.** Currently, students who participate in in-firm learning tend to receive on-site class-room training, observe the work of actual employees, or engage in practical activities that are separate from the actual production process. None of these activities generate direct benefits for the employer. To an extent, the lack of participation in the production process of students is due to the generally short duration of in-firm learning that is currently practices (box 3.7)

- **Employers appear to not take into account all potential medium and longer term benefits of WBL, including in the context of demographic trends.** A lack, among some firms, of medium and longer term planning, implies that they do not take into account that their participation in WBL contributes to creating a larger pool of qualified labor. This reduces the perceived benefits of engaging in WBL, even though this is a particularly pertinent aspect to take into account particularly in the Polish context of low labor participation rates combined with an ageing population

- **WBL engagement tends to be insufficiently marketed to have a noticeable impact on a firm's image.** There are, nevertheless, some examples of activities which can contribute to increase incentives for firms' participation in WBL through messaging to the broader public. For example, since 2015, the mayor's office in Starachowice awards the "Iron Ring" prize for contributions to regional economic development, which could potentially include enterprises providing good examples of WBL.

In addition to specific capacity constraints of firms in the area of WBL, other aspects affect firms' willingness and ability to engage in WBL:

- **Enterprises do not necessarily consider VET providers as sound partners** who are willing and able to acknowledge and help respond to firms' preferences and constraints; who can provide reliable plans on the number of students that are available for WBL for pre-defined periods; and who are able to offer stable, systematic interactions between teachers and enterprise staff. Lack of trust in VET providers is partly due to previous experiences of school-firm collaboration which were less than successful, and makes (some) firms reluctant to engage in WBL activities.[5] The lack of a culture in which firm-school collaboration is formalized through a clear contract or other form of cooperation agreement, accompanied by mechanisms to monitor and ensure compliance with the content of such documents, may contribute to this situation.
- **Enterprises have little experience in skill development activities, even of their own employees.** For example, only 22 percent of firms are reported to invest in training provision of their employees, compared to the EU average of 66 percent (Eurostat 2017).

Increasing the direct benefits of WBL-provision for firms

Firms generate direct benefits from WBL when students participate in the enterprises' production processes. Students' productivity is assumed to increase as they spend a longer time in the firm, since this allows them to gradually acquire more relevant knowledge and skills to independently carry out required production activities. Direct benefits are off-set by direct costs in terms of wages or remuneration that are paid to the WBL-students. Kis (2016) provides a model to assess the firms' direct benefits of WBL engagement taking into account variables such as the WBL period, student remuneration, and amount of public subsidy (figure B3.7.1).

Consultations have shown that firms in Świętokrzyskie tend not to engage WBL-students in actual production activities, thereby making it impossible to generate direct benefits from WBL. Instead, firms consider the benefits of WBL to be limited to 1) responding to skills shortages by training students in occupations and competences that are needed in the workplace; and 2) lowering the costs of recruitment and preparatory training. This is in response to circumstances where firms, especially those outside big agglomerations, find it increasingly hard to attract sufficiently skilled workers, if not due to increasing labor demand, then at least to replace the large shares of retiring employees. In addition to recruiting qualified immigrants, for example, from Ukraine and Belarus, companies seek future employees in vocational schools.

Even when the direct benefits of WBL are not firms' main objective to engage in WBL, engaging students in production processes would be beneficial since (1) it is expected to be among the most effective approaches to skills development through WBL; and (2) it would increase firms' willingness to engage in WBL by its impact on the cost-benefit ratio.

Promoting student engagement in production processes is expected to require a combination of activities, including extending the duration of WBL periods (allowing sufficient time to increase students' productivity); support measures to build firm capacity to integrate students in production processes; and additional measures that reduce firms' costs to engage in WBL provision (which could

continued

Box 3.7, *continued*

comprise a mix of further capacity building and tools development, and financial incentives). One aspect raised particularly by firms in the heavy industry sector that would need to be addressed, relates to exposing students to heavy machinery in a way that both reduces safety concerns and the risk of financial losses in case equipment gets damaged.

FIGURE B3.7.1

A stylized model of trainee productivity

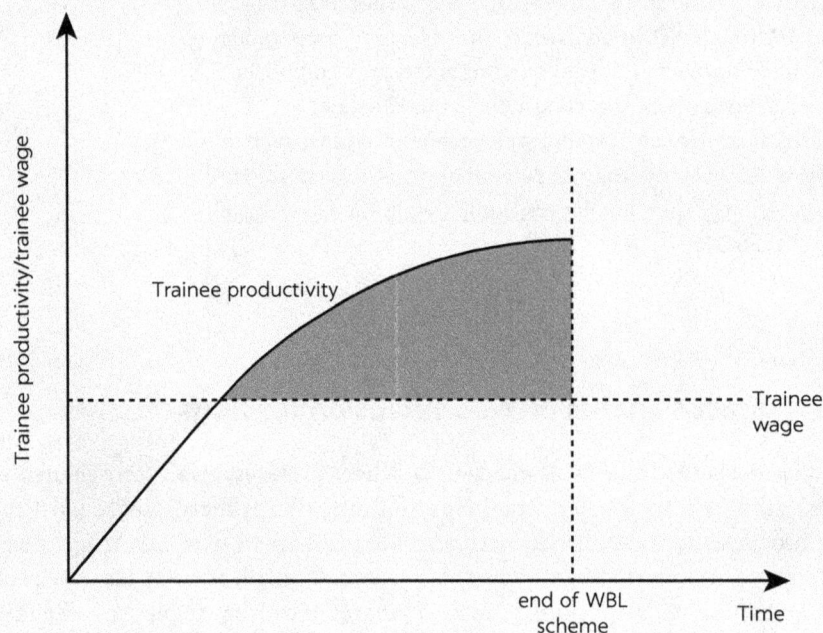

Source: Kis 2016.

International practices

Across Europe, a plethora initiatives are being implemented to incentivize and support firms in offering sound WBL.[6] Generally, the mechanisms in place aim to address constraints that also apply to firms in Świętokrzyskie. Incentives and support tend to be provided by the government, the social partners, or both. The wide range of arrangements that are applied internationally can be categorized in those that are financial (such as subsidies and tax-breaks) and those that are non-financial, such as adjustments in the design of the WBL format or processes to make them more attractive to employers. A recent OECD Working Paper focusing on apprenticeships finds that, while financial support is common, its impact can be modest and can depend on both the amount of financial support and allocation criteria; schemes targeting specific sectors and that are supported by social partners tend to be more successful. The paper finds that non-financial measures tend to be less costly than financial support, and can also increase the provision of apprenticeships (Kuczera 2017). Examples include:

- **Financial measures:** the amount and source of financing that firms which offer WBL placements receive differs substantially across countries. For example, in Norway, firms receive a substantial subsidy from government funds, while the government of Switzerland does not provide a subsidy. In Denmark, an employer levy finances the wage of apprentices when they receive their off-the-job training in vocational schools. In England, a newly introduced employer levy is intended to fund the off-the-job training and assessment received by apprentices, but it does not directly subsidize employers. In Austria, several sectors have established voluntary training funds that provide compensation to firms participating in WBL (box 3.8).

- **Capacity**: In Austria, guidance material on WBL provision is provided to firms (online and in print) by the Chamber of Commerce and the Ministry of Economy (ReferNet 2014a). In Norway, "training offices" particularly support small and medium enterprises (SMEs) in managing and implementing WBL, among others through carrying out various administrative responsibilities and coaching enterprise staff in the tutoring of apprentices (ReferNet 2014c). In Germany, the Federal Institute for Vocational Education and Training develop extensive implementation guides on new initial vocational training programs, to assist VET practitioners (BIBB 2014) (box 3.9).

- **Teaching methods and pedagogical skills**: in Finland, the National Board of Education has developed a program specifically for workplace instructors within the national qualification framework (box 3.10). The training is targeted specifically at enterprise employees who will train or supervise students in firms (rather then, for example, at VET teachers who are employed in schools).[7] In Germany, the Federal Institute for Vocational Education and Training (BIBB) operates a website designed for in-company trainers (see www.foraus.de). In Spain, EU-funding financed the development of a practical guide for transversal skills of in-company trainers, concentrating on the different roles that trainers have in their companies, the competencies required for each of them, and approaches to combine varying responsibilities (DualVet 2015).

- **Marketing WBL engagement**: to generate positive publicity for firms engaging in WBL, the Ministry of Economy in Austria allocates awards to firms with special achievements in apprenticeship training (box 3.11).

BOX 3.8

Austria—sectoral training funds

Several voluntary company-supported sectoral training funds have been established in Austria, including for example the regional fund for the electrical and metal industry in Vorarlberg, and (nationwide) in the construction industry.

The Vorarlberg electrical and metal industry (VEM) introduced a training fund in 1978. Funds are raises through a levy on gross wages (initially set at 1.5 per 1,000, currently 2.4 per 1,000). The funds provide "support premiums," which are paid to companies providing apprenticeship training, based on the performance of young people in annually-held apprenticeship skills competitions. Another part of the funds is used to finance career guidance activities and training courses for in-firm instructors, as well as language courses for the apprentices and trainers.

In addition to increasing incentives for engaging in work-based learning (WBL), the shared responsibility across firms in a particular sector of the costs of WBL provision also addresses the "public-aspects" of WBL provision by individual firms.[a]

Source: Petanovitsch, Kurt, and Wolfgang 2014.
a. The public-good aspects of WBL relate to fact that students who are trained in a particular firm, might end up working for another firm, implying that the firm which provides WBL may not be the one benefitting from it. The sector approach to financing WBL results in a sharing of the costs of WBL by all firms who might benefit from it.

BOX 3.9

Germany—implementation guides

During the process of revising the training regulations, employers' representatives and trade unions requested the BIBB (the Federal Institute for Vocational Education and Training) to develop implementation guides on the new initial vocational training programs to assist VET practitioners.

The "Structuring Training" (*Ausbildung gestalten*) series of guides issued by BIBB offer support concerning the implementation of new vocational training regulations. It provides guidance for companies, part-time vocational schools, inter-company training centers, competent bodies, and apprentices.

The publications describe and explain new provisions in detail, and contain an extensive commentary on each provision of the regulation in question. Explanatory notes on the learning objectives targeted by the general training plan provide illustrative examples of the training content. The skills, knowledge and capabilities to be taught are exemplified in terms of concrete learning projects and assignments to

facilitate the trainers' task of delivering the specified training. Practical examples of the structure of intermediate and final examinations for new or updated occupations offer tips for trainers, examiners and even trainees.

Tips for planning vocational training—such as checklists for the training company, explanatory notes on developing an in-house training plan and examples of training logs help everyone involved in initial vocational training. The training profile and framework curriculum for classroom instruction at part-time vocational school are included for information purposes. The explanatory notes and guides for day-to-day VET practice are supplemented by information about possible continuing training programs and qualifications in the respective occupation, and suggestions for further reading.

Implementation guides have been issued for around 150 new or updated training occupations in recent years.

Source: BIBB 2014.

BOX 3.10

Finland—workplace instructor training within the national qualifications framework

The Finnish National Board of Education developed a program for workplace instructor training, with the achievement of learning outcomes targeted by this program accounting for three credits under the National Qualifications Framework (NQF). The program is competency-based and includes learning outcomes. The program documentation also includes examples of how training content can be covered and studied; background materials for designing instructional materials; and information on various training methods and models. Some examples of the program material are provided in figures B3.10.1 and B3.10.2 below.

The training accounts for 3 credits within the NQF (corresponding to an estimated 3 weeks to complete the training), and comprises of 3 modules (of 1-credit each) that can be taken separately and in any order:

1. Planning of training provided at the workplace, demonstration of vocational skills, and competence tests
2. Instructing the student and assessing learning
3. Assessing the student's or candidate's competences.

While Finnish regulations do not make completion of this training obligatory, education providers who

continued

Box 3.10, *continued*

engage with firms on WBL can recommend completion of the training as a prerequisite to acting as a workplace instructor. The importance of training for workplace instructors can be highlighted during negotiations on collaboration.

Education providers who collaborate with enterprises can arrange workplace instructor training themselves. They can also implement such training in cooperation with other education providers (e.g., at the regional level), or arrange for the training provision by for example institutions that provide continuing education. Workplace instructor training implemented at the regional level has yielded positive results, among others because this approach ensures consistency of training across firms in the region.

Funding sources for the training can be varied, and tend to include education providers, firms, and state funding. Support granted by the European Social Fund has also been applied to train workplace instructors involved in WBL for students of upper secondary VET, as well as for the development of the training program.

Examples of training program documentation:

FIGURE B3.10.1

Criteria for organizing workplace instructor training (excerpt)

CRITERIA	Not fulfilled	Partly fulfilled	Fulfilled	Grounds
Planning of training				
1. The recommendation on Training for Workplace Instructors, 3 credits (Finnish National Board of Education 2012) is used as a basis for the planning of training.				
2. Training is jointly planned by teachers and workplace instructors.				
3. Planning takes account of participants' existing skills and knowledge.				
Marketing and communication activities related to training				
4. Marketing and communication activities related to training are executed in a systematic manner.				
5. Various marketing channels and tools are used in the marketing of such training.				
6. Communication and marketing efforts reach the right target group.				
Method of organising training				
7. Organisation of training is workplace-oriented.				
8. From the participants' perspective, training is flexible.				
Content of training				
9. Training content complies with the recommendation on training for workplace instructors, 3 credits: 1. Planning of training provided at the workplace, vocational skills demonstrations and competence tests (1 credit) 2. Instructing the student and assessing learning (1 credit)				

Source: Lammi 2014.

continued

Box 3.10, *continued*

FIGURE B3.10.2

Structuring the training process: an example

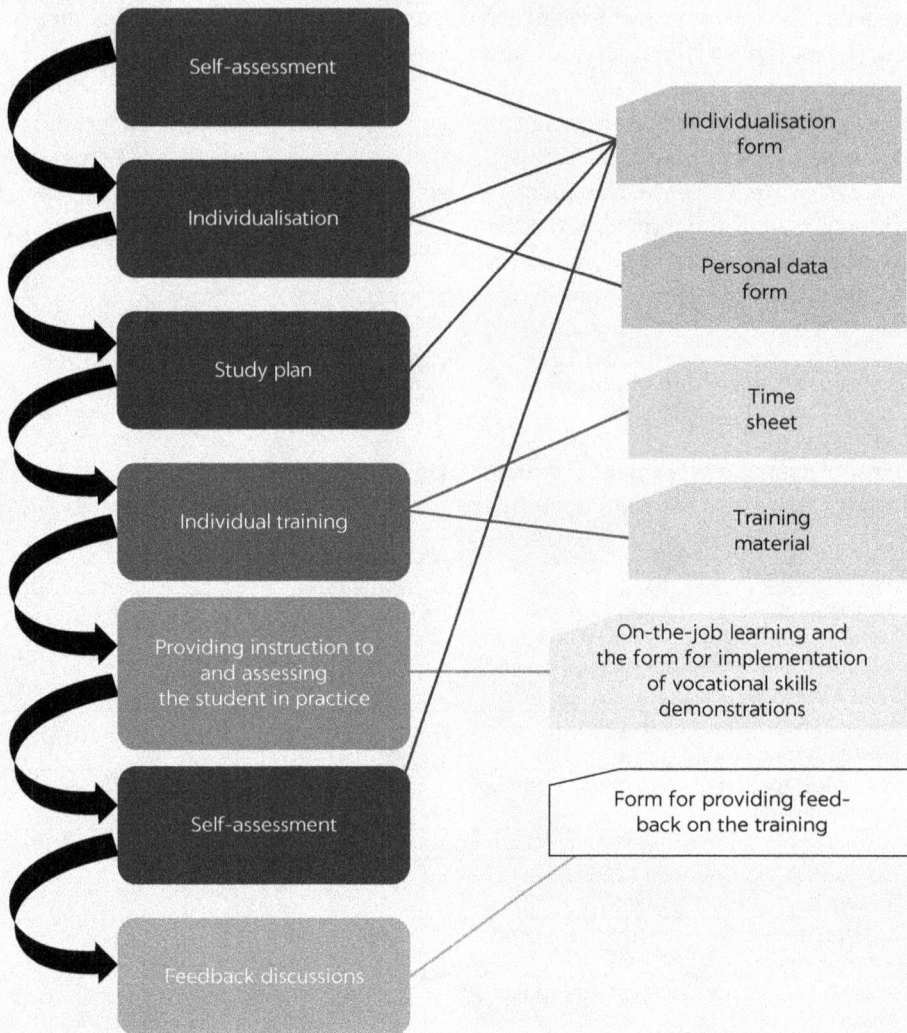

Source: Lammi 2014.

BOX 3.11

Austria—company awards for strong performance in apprenticeships

The Austrian Minister of Economy awards various prizes to companies with strong performance in apprenticeship provision.

The "State-honored training company" award is given to training companies for special achievements in apprenticeship training. Criteria for awarding the

continued

Box 3.11, *continued*

state prize include: success in apprenticeship-leave exams and in provincial and national competitions; dedicated involvement in the field of career guidance; cooperation ventures entered into by the training company; and its in-house and external CET programs for apprentices and trainers. Applications for this award are submitted to the regional advisory board on apprenticeship that is set up at the apprenticeship office of the respective province.

The "Best training companies—Fit for future" prize is awarded every two years, in the categories of small, medium-sized and large enterprises. The objective of

the state prize is to improve quality, innovation and sustainability in apprenticeship training. Specifically, the state prize aims to

- set a clear signal for quality in apprenticeship
- acknowledge the excellent work of the Austrian economy in the field of youth training
- help win over new companies for apprenticeship training and
- raise awareness among parents and youths of the good training provided in Austrian companies and the wide spectrum of apprenticeship occupations.

Source: Federal Ministry of Economy, Family and Youth 2014.

Applications for Świętokrzyskie

Firms' constraints related to incentives and to capacity are reinforcing determinants of sound WBL provision. On the one hand, weak capacity increases the costs of WBL provision which reduces firms' incentives to engage in WBL. On the other hand, lacking incentives for WBL provision reduce the motivation of enterprises to build knowledge and capacity for its provision. Constraints related to incentives and to capacity could therefore ideally addressed simultaneously.

On the short term, funding schemes that are initiated, managed, and financed by the private sector are unlikely to emerge. Considering the low degree of organization of the private sector, combined with their low confidence in the possibility to implement WBL effectively, the establishment of a financing scheme for WBL is likely to require engagement and funding from other stakeholders, including particularly government actors. Once trust in the WBL approach increases, and ideally collaboration among firms strengthens, both the appetite and ability of the private sector to manage and finance WBL could be expected to increase.

With numerous examples of mechanisms to support firms in WBL implementation available, a pragmatic approach to identifying schemes that are considered workable within the Świętokrzyskie context, may be advisable. Considering the weak capacity and financial constraints among all stakeholders, the region might want to opt for approaches that require relatively limited efforts and resources. For example, developing information and guidance material for WBL implementation and training of workplace instructors, and ensuring their online dissemination, may be a more feasible approach than aiming to establish an extensive and costly network of apprenticeship liaisons. Rewarding firms with strong WBL performance through awards ceremonies could be considered a cost-effective and relatively easy-to-implement approach to generating publicity and to incentivizing firms to increase their engagement in WBL.

The pilot project will test approaches and generate lessons learned on appropriate methods to attract enterprises to engage in WBL and to promote in-firm learning. The approaches that are expected to be applied during the pilot project include providing training to workplace instructors, guidance on how to engage VET students in actual production processes, and financial compensation.

PRIORITY DIMENSION 5: QUALITY ASSURANCE MECHANISMS FOR WBL

Quality assurance is a key part of a strong WBL system, aiming to ensure that all stakeholders have a justified confidence in the knowledge and skills acquired through training. The formal completion of training, of which WBL is an integral part, should be interpreted by labor market actors as a signal that graduates are equipped with the appropriate and required knowledge, skills and competencies. It thus serves to assure students of the quality of the training that they invest in; companies of the quality of their (potential) employees; and trainers (both VET schools and firms engaged in WBL) of the quality of their training provision.

Quality assurance of WBL serves to guarantee the achievement of appropriate learning outcomes by students during their in-firm experiences, irrespective of the firm where the WBL takes place. Achieving an appropriate quality of WBL is a shared responsibility of all key stakeholders involved: firms, VET providers, and students.[8]

Areas for improvement

The QA system for VET in Poland is somewhat outdated, and hardly geared toward assuring the quality of WBL provision. A principle mechanism for QA is the pedagogical supervision system, carried out by educational superintendents, which tends not to focus on achieving demand-responsive learning outcomes of students, but rather concentrates on assessing compliance with regulations related to, for example, the required formal qualifications of teachers; the inclusion of required learning outcomes in curricula; and the presence of teaching aids in classrooms in all the necessary teaching aids. In addition, external examinations (carried out by regional examination boards) are a key element in schools' accountability. As a result, VET providers "teach to the test", and are unlikely to be very motivated to increase the incidence and duration of WBL, unless the learning outcomes that can be expected to be achieved in firms are incorporated in the examinations.

No regulations or clear guidance is made available to firms and schools to guide them in carrying out sound quality assurance of WBL. Regulations related to VET provision do not address the specificities of QA in WBL. In addition, no support structures or effective knowledge exchange mechanisms exist in the region to build capacity of schools or firms in the area of QA for WBL.

While several firms and VET providers report to apply QA tools for WBL, there are concerns about their validity. For example, some schools report using traineeship diaries, in which practical training teachers or instructors record information on completed elements of in-firm training, including sometimes assigning grades and providing feedback on student's work. In other instances, school staff conduct a post-WBL conversation with students to review whether the WBL experience was completed and whether students have achieved planned learning outcomes. Other VET providers review learning outcomes achieved through WBL through a written test. While these are certainly all steps in the right direction, there is no evidence of the "quality of the quality assurance mechanisms,"[9] and hence of their positive impact on WBL learning outcomes.

International practices

International practices highlight that the quality of WBL provision is taken into account at various stages of the WBL process, from moment when firms are considered for WBL provision, until the final examination of VET graduates. In particular, quality considerations come into play when:

- Identifying firms and assessing their capacity to provide WBL
- Assuring the competences of in-firm tutors and trainers
- Assuring effective collaboration between firms and VET providers on WBL provision
- Assuring a proper organization of WBL in firms
- Identifying those learning outcomes incorporated in the curriculum that should be achieved through WBL
- Assessing learning outcomes achieved through WBL
- Ensuring that learning outcomes achieved through WBL are adequately covered in (final) examinations.

The European Quality Assurance in Vocational Education and Training (EQAVET) Network has identified six "building blocks" that are commonly applied for QA in WBL across countries. As is indicated in figure 3.2 below, these building blocks range from an early consideration of QA during the early stages of WBL planning, to measures to ensure quality during WBL provision and, finally to an adequate assessment of learning outcomes (EQAVET 2012).

A varied collection of QA measures is applied in EU member states with strong WBL systems. These include the screening of firms before they engage in WBL; self-evaluation tools for firms; clear training plans; student education portfolio's; and WBL monitoring mechanisms that help direct support to firms who most need it. Specific examples are provided below.

- **Firm screening and accreditation:** Firms in Austria, before they may offer apprenticeships, need to be accredited by the relevant Apprenticeship Office in collaboration with the Chamber of Labor, which assess compliance of the firm with legal and company-specific prerequisites (Petanovitsch, Kurt, and Wolfgang 2014). In Belgium, assessing readiness for apprenticeship provision in the hospitality sector is the responsibility of *Horeca Vorming Vlaanderen* (HVV, Hospitality Training Flanders), established by the social partners in the sectors to promote skill development. HVV assesses and accredits firms for WBL based on a set of criteria established to ensure that firms can adequately contribute to the acquisition of skills that are included in the sector's competency profiles (which are also developed by HVV). This assessment includes the placement of a teacher in the firm to experience a "mock internship" (European Commission 2013). In the Netherlands, sector-specific "Centers of Expertise" play a key role in firm screening, among other QA activities (box 3.12).

FIGURE 3.2

Building blocks for effective quality assurance of work-based learning

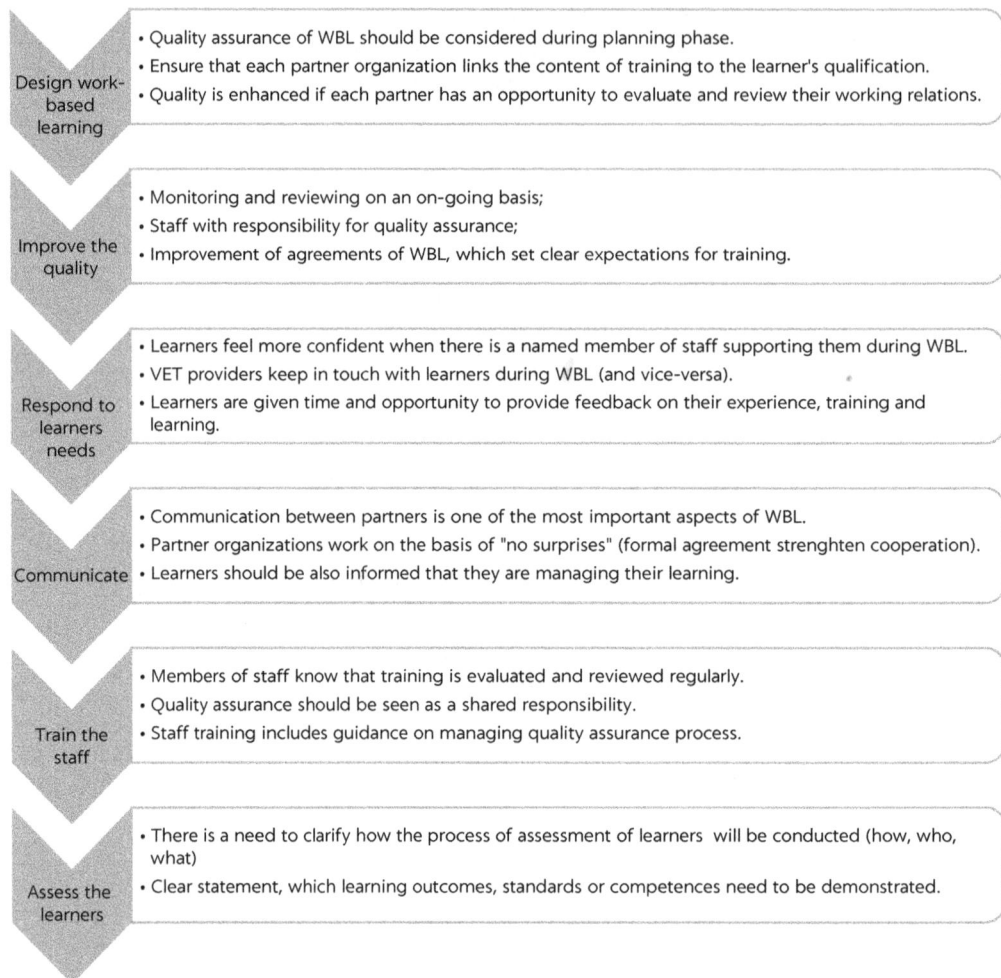

Design work-based learning	• Quality assurance of WBL should be considered during planning phase. • Ensure that each partner organization links the content of training to the learner's qualification. • Quality is enhanced if each partner has an opportunity to evaluate and review their working relations.
Improve the quality	• Monitoring and reviewing on an on-going basis; • Staff with responsibility for quality assurance; • Improvement of agreements of WBL, which set clear expectations for training.
Respond to learners needs	• Learners feel more confident when there is a named member of staff supporting them during WBL. • VET providers keep in touch with learners during WBL (and vice-versa). • Learners are given time and opportunity to provide feedback on their experience, training and learning.
Communicate	• Communication between partners is one of the most important aspects of WBL. • Partner organizations work on the basis of "no surprises" (formal agreement strenghten cooperation). • Learners should be also informed that they are managing their learning.
Train the staff	• Members of staff know that training is evaluated and reviewed regularly. • Quality assurance should be seen as a shared responsibility. • Staff training includes guidance on managing quality assurance process.
Assess the learners	• There is a need to clarify how the process of assessment of learners will be conducted (how, who, what) • Clear statement, which learning outcomes, standards or competences need to be demonstrated.

Source: EQAVET 2012.

- **Self-evaluation of firms:** In Switzerland, tools allowing firms to self-evaluate their strengths and weaknesses related to WBL provision are in place alongside a formal licensing system (box 3.13).
- **Clear training plans and contracts:** In Norway, a clear description of the objectives and scope of WBL is included in a mandatory contract that is signed by the student, firm, and VET provider; the contract also specifies the student's trainer or supervisor (ReferNet 2014c). In Germany, detailed in-company training plans are developed for each student (box 3.14).
- **Student education portfolio:** in Denmark, in addition to the development of individual education plans, students maintain a "personal education portfolio" intended, among others, to increase their awareness of the learning process (box 3.15).
- **Monitoring WBL performance of firms:** In Austria, social partners monitor WBL performance based on a set of annually evaluated indicators, and use the findings to target support activities to firms which have relatively weak performance (box 3.16).

BOX 3.12

The Netherlands—firm accreditation by the Cooperation Organisation for Vocational Education, Training, and the Labour Market

The Dutch Cooperation Organization for Vocational Education, Training, and the Labor Market (*Samenwerkingsorganisatie Beroepsonderwijs Bedrijfsleven*, SBB) is a collaboration of VET providers and the private sector, aimed at improving employability of VET students and aligning skill supply with demand through work placements. The SBB has a legal mandate for accrediting and coaching work placement companies; maintaining the qualification framework for secondary vocational education; and providing labor market information, including on professional practical training and the adequacy of VET provision. In addition, the SBB advises the Ministries of Education and of Economic Affairs on the alignment of VET provision with labor demand. The SBB works on a sector, regional and national level, and replaces the previous Sectoral Centers of Excellence, which carried out similar tasks as the SBB until 2015.

The SBB's accreditation criteria serve to determine the if the quality of the work placement is suitable for appropriate skill acquisition, and if the firm offers a good and safe working and learning environment with appropriate supervision.

The accreditation is based on common quality criteria, related among others to:

- Training opportunities
- Experienced and competent in-house trainer

- Preparation to cooperation with school, including regular contacts between work-place trainer with school
- Availability of work space for students.

Upon accreditation, firms receive support from the SBB. For example, SBBs facilitate training provision for in-firm trainers, communication with schools, student recruitment (publishing information on the web page), and knowledge exchanges between companies.

In 2013 and 2014, Centers of Excellence (the predecessors of the SBB) accredited 10.000 companies for WBL placements. Notably, around 8.200 of these firms had not been involved in VET before, and 1.200 firms were accredited for—to them—new qualifications. On the other hand, 9,200 accredited companies withdrew in this period because of the lack of staff to coach learners due to the economic crises.

Accredited work-places are registered on an open website, facilitating students and schools in finding work placement.

Quality of WBL placement is monitored by education advisers, who regularly visit work places, conducting monitoring as well as providing advice for all key actors in all aspects of work-based learning.

Sources: https://www.s-bb.nl/en; European Commission 2013; ReferNet 2014d.

BOX 3.13

Switzerland—the QualiCarte self-evaluation of WBL

The QualiCarte was introduced in 2006 through a collaboration between cantonal governments and social partners. The QualiCarte allows firms to perform a self-evaluation of the education process. Among others, the QualiCarte tool allows firms to:

- Recognize the improvement potential of their own training performance
- Sustainably improve training quality

- Increase the attractiveness of its own company as a training enterprise
- Optimize the selection of trainees
- Minimize the risk of discontinued training
- Evaluate the quality and relevance of work-based learning (WBL) provided by the firm
- Obtain support in acquiring an education license.

Sources: Petanovitsch, Kurt, and Wolfgang 2014; http://www.berufsbildung.ch/dyn/4695.aspx.

BOX 3.14

Germany—in-company training plans

In-company training plans define the "factual" and "chronological" structure of the in-firm learning experience of a WBL student in a particular firm. The training plans are developed by the company, based on the framework training plan, i.e. the syllabus and timetable that are incorporated in the training regulation. The training plan is based on the firm's infrastructure and work-processes, and provides an indicative timeframe of topics that have to be covered over the duration of the apprenticeship. With the in-company training plan, the apprentice and the firm staff agree on the allocation of learning objectives in time sequences.

The factual structure of the training plan relates to the knowledge and skills defined in the training regulations for the respective occupation profile (divided in different training units). The chronological structure describes the time that will be dedicated to particular subjects and training units. The training plan includes a description of the machines, tools and working places that the firm should provide. In addition, the different training segments have to be included: courses, school and company and—as the first training segment—the trial period.

According to regulations, the factual and chronological structure of the training plan should include the following

Factual structure:

- Must contain all skills and knowledge included in the training regulations
- Skills and knowledge that a student will acquire should be summarized in "training units," with a clear indication of which functions or departments within the firm are responsible for each unit
- The content of the training units should be easy to grasp
- For the whole training program and for each individual training unit, training will start with teaching basic knowledge and skills, followed by more advanced and specialized skills and knowledge
- The factual structure must take into account the demands of intermediate and final examinations.

Chronological structure

- Should be within the scope of the contractual training period
- Should take into account the factual and pedagogical aspects of training
- Has to consider the order of the examinations
- Has to adhere by any chronological sequences that are prescribed in training regulations
- Should include clear segments with a maximum duration of six months and may define subsegments
- Can be flexible; for example, segments can be shortened or extended depending on the needs of the trainee.

In the below publication (DualVet 2015, 159), there is an exemplary training plan.

Sources: DualVet 2015; Apprenticeship Toolbox, In-Company Training in Germany (www.apprenticeship-toolbox.eu).

BOX 3.15

Denmark—personal educational portfolio

In addition to an educational plan, students maintain a personal educational portfolio. Recognizing that the impact of an alternating school-company learning program depends not only on the quality of the different parts, but also on how these parts interact, the education portfolio connects and combines

continued

Box 3.15, *continued*

documentation on study sequences and learning outcomes. Moreover, the students' responsibility in developing the portfolio aims to increase their awareness of the learning process, and empower them to be their own "learning agent."

Specifically, the education portfolio intends to serve the following purposes:

- Ensure that the student has a good overview of his or her overall education
- Document student and learning achievement in the various elements of the program
- Enhance awareness among students and firms on the function of WBL as an integral part of learning in VET

- Facilitate content-related coordination of college teaching and practical in-company training.

The education portfolio must contain the personal education plan, VET college recommendations and VET college examination documents, as well as a description of the qualifications and competencies achieved by the student during the overall learning process in college and company. Furthermore, the portfolio must include ministerial orders and the specific course regulation pertaining to the course as well as a copy of the apprenticeship contract.

The college is responsible for handing over an educational portfolio to each student. The document is owned by the student.

Sources: Danish Ministry of Education 2000; ReferNet 2014b.

BOX 3.16

Austria—quality management of apprenticeships through sound monitoring systems

The Quality Management in Apprenticeship (*Qualitätsmanagement Lehrlingsausbildung, QML*) initiative was launched in 2013 by the social partners. Its goal is to increase the number of young people who complete an apprenticeship and pass the apprenticeship examination—without lowering the level of the exam. QML builds on a set of annually evaluated indicators of apprenticeship dropouts, the number of apprentices who (do not) sit for the final exam as well as the number of apprentices who do (or do not) acquire the apprenticeship certificate.

In the initial phase of this data-based quality assurance scheme, the focus is on apprenticeships where the worst indicators are found. More in-depth analyses are conducted for the apprenticeships concerned to identify the causes as far as possible. Some of these causes are expected to include:

- topicality and quality of in-company training curricula/training regulations

- the suitability of apprentices
- the training companies' degree of specialization and equipment
- the quality of in-company training (IVET trainers, the planning of training, etc.) and
- the quality of complementary training provided at part-time vocational school, etc.

The analysis and interpretation of these indicators form the basis for quality assurance and improvement measures, such as:

- the adjustment of in-company training curricula
- improvement of career guidance
- measures supporting apprentices (such as remedial lessons, coaching)
- train-the-trainer programs
- supporting materials for training companies
- improvements in the apprenticeship-leave exams, etc.

Source: ReferNet 2014a.

Countries with recognized well-established WBL mechanisms tend to apply a variety of quality assurance and improvement mechanisms covering preparation, implementation, and evaluation phases of WBL. Apart from solutions tackling particular problems, those countries introduce a general approach that promotes quality culture. A good example is Austria's VET Quality Initiative (QIBB), which was launched in 2004 as a voluntary initiative and became obligatory in 2011. It embraces all the principles of quality management: the plan-do-check-act cycle of constant improvement, the self-evaluation as basic means of assuring quality, and involvement of all stakeholders. The general approach is accompanied by concrete instruments and solutions that are available for firms and VET providers.[10]

Applications for Świętokrzyskie

Considering the weak QA culture and the absence of effective oversight and support mechanisms for WBL in Świętokrzyskie, an approach that "starts small and expands gradually" appears appropriate for the region. For example, while eventually a formal accreditation mechanism for firms that engage in WBL may be appropriate, there is currently no credible institution that could ensure its implementation, and it might deter firms' willingness to participate in WBL. Similarly, establishing an elaborate WBL support system where "WBL-advisors" provide relatively intensive tailor-made support to individual firms may be unfeasible in the short term, given (among others) the financial constraints facing the VET sector. Moreover, the international practices described above are applied in countries where WBL comprises an extensive element of VET provision whereas in Poland, on the other hand, the WBL component of technical education is still limited. Options that therefore appear more feasible and appropriate are those that require relatively limited resources and institutional capacity, and that do not pose a discouraging burden on employers. These could include, for example, the development and online dissemination of tools and templates, including for (self-) evaluation of firm readiness to provide WBL, preparing WBL training plans, and guiding students in the preparation of education portfolios.

The pilot project on Implementation of Work-Based Learning in Świętokrzyskie will develop an initial set of QA tools and templates. Supported by technical assistance that is part of the project, the tools and/or templates to be developed will aim to support those QA mechanisms that are considered most appropriate by regional stakeholders. Project beneficiaries will be engaged in the development of the tools and will receive support to apply them. The tools are expected to be fine-tuned during project implementation, and subsequently be made available to a wider public. Key tools that will be developed are expected to include guidance and templates on the determination and assessment of learning outcomes that are to be achieved through WBL (in line with the core curriculum).

PRIORITY DIMENSION 6: A FACILITATING ROLE FOR CENTERS FOR PRACTICAL TRAINING

There are various instances in which "work-floor simulating environments" are considered a viable alternative for in-firm learning. When in-firm training is either not available, or not considered appropriate given student's learning needs or skill level, practical learning in workshops or laboratories that are managed by schools or related entities can either replace of prepare students for in-firm training. In particular, work-floor simulating environments can be suitable when:

- They are made available to students who did not manage to find a company for WBL
- They serve to provide students with skills that prepare them for in-firm WBL (for example, to prepare students to work safely and adequately with highly complicated or expensive equipment)
- They complement in-firm learning, for example by teaching particular skills that cannot be appropriately acquired through in-firm training
- They are used to conduct assessments of learning outcomes of WBL.

Work-floor simulating environments need to equip VET students with job-relevant skills, in conjunction with practical skill acquisition through in-firm WBL. This implies that those stakeholders that are responsible for providing training through work-floor simulating environments should be able to identify and respond to private sector skill demand, as well as ensure that training provision in these environments is aligned (rather than in competition) with practical training that is provided in firms.

Areas for improvement

Centers for Practical Training (CPT) appear to crowd-out employer-based traineeships, and are likely to discourage practical activities from taking place in firms. Figure 3.3 below depicts the location at which traineeships take place in a selected number of *poviats* in Świętokrzyskie. In the two *poviats* which have established CPTs (Skarzysko-Kamienna and Starachowice), the share of students who carry out traineeships with employers is 87 percent and 84 percent, respectively. This is substantially less than in the other *poviats*, where the share ranges from 91 percent to 100 percent, and well below the regional average of 90 percent. This can be considered as an indication that the presence of CPTs reduces the likelihood that students carry out their traineeship in firms, even though these are required by the national legislation to take place with employers.[11]

FIGURE 3.3

Location of traineeships in technical education (share of students, selected Świętokrzyskie *poviats*)

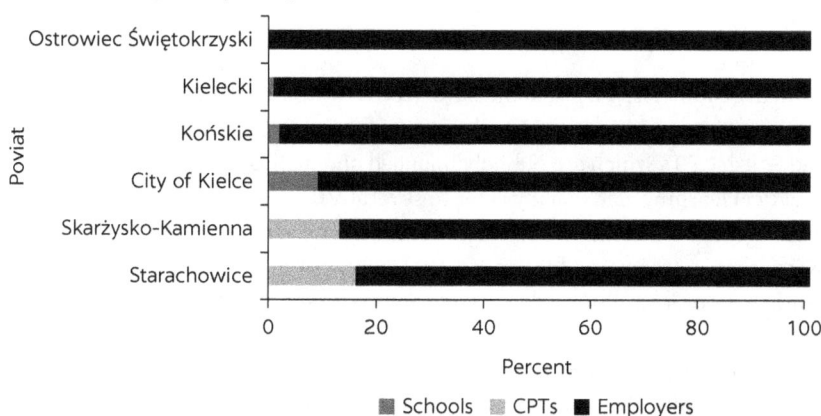

Sources: MoNE Education Information System; World Bank.
Note: CPT = Center for Practical Training.

Since the share of technical students who carry out practical activities (rather than traineeships) in firms is very low in all *poviats*, data do not show that CPTs crowd-out the provision of practical activities of firms; rather, CPT-based training replaces training that was previously provided in schools. However, it appears safe to assume that, also in the case of practical activities, the presence of CPTs creates a disincentive to seek opportunities to arrange these activities with employers.

Elements of ESF interventions may increase incentives to provide training in CPTs, rather than in firms. In the past years, VET in Poland received significant EU financing, in particular from the ESF and the European Regional Development Fund (ERDF). As these funds were partially allocated to purchase equipment for CPTs, the system to monitor the performance of these financing mechanisms includes indicators related to the use of this equipment.[12] While this is an understandable approach considering the need to assess the efficient use of funding, these indicators create incentives for training provision in CPTs rather than in firms, and thus are likely to discourage efforts to increase the incidence and duration of WBL.

Mechanisms to ensure that training provision in CPTs is demand-responsive tend to be weak. Whereas generally CPT management aims to align training provision with skill demand, available mechanisms to achieve this goal are not fully exploited. For example, in various CPTs, efforts to align training provision with skill demand do include communications with enterprises. However, more structural mechanisms to ensure that training provision is demand-driven appear to be rare or absent. For example, during regional consultations, no examples were identified of CPTs which are managed by a board comprising a majority (or even some) private sector representatives, or where the private sector co-finances CPTs.

It is unclear to what extent CPTs succeed in simulating actual working environments. A key assumed advantage of WBL is that, in addition to learning relevant technical skills, exposure to a real-world working environment, and its diverse challenges, equips students with non-technical skills related to team work, discipline, problem solving, and handling conflicts. In principle, workplace simulations in CPTs might (to a degree) equip students with such skills, for example through project-based and team-based learning approaches. While an in-depth assessment of learning approaches in CPTs is not available it appears, however, that they concentrate mostly on teaching technical skills.

International practices

In many countries, VET schools have access to workshops and laboratories to equip students with practical skills outside for firms. However, institutions like the Polish CPTs which are publicly financed and managed, focus exclusively on practical learning, and usually cater to several VET providers, are rare in countries with well-established WBL mechanisms. In countries such as the Netherlands, Ireland and Germany, VET schools typically maintain their own workshops or laboratories, designed to equip students with basic practical skills before they start WBL experiences. These workshops tend to be an integrated part of VET schools. Sometimes employers, for example in Germany, may individually or collectively own and maintain a training workshop where apprentices learn the basics of their trade before starting work, still as apprentices, on the productive side; the distinctive feature of CPTs is their existence in the public sector, but separate from VET schools.

Institutions to address a lack of appropriate WBL placements in enterprises tend to focus on promoting firm collaboration and supporting students in finding placements, sometimes complemented by practical training provision outside of firms. In Austria and Germany, in case a firm is unable to ensure that a WBL-student achieves all necessary learning outcomes, initiatives exist to promote collaboration between this firm and other enterprises or with training providers. In Denmark, Centers of Placement, in addition to supporting students in identifying WBL places in firms, provide practical learning to students for whom in-firm placements were not available (box 3.17–3.19).

BOX 3.17

Austria—training alliances

There are two types of training alliances in Austria: compulsory and voluntary, and different options to organize the training (figure B3.17.1).

If a company is unable to provide all skills and know-how required for a particular apprenticeship, then the Austrian Vocational Training Act obliges the provision of additional learning experiences outside of the firm through the formation of a training alliance. In this case, supplementary training measures are provided by another appropriate company or suitable training establishment (for example, adult education providers). The content of the training that is provided outside the firm that is offering the WBL placement, as well as the "alliance partner," are agreed in the apprenticeship contract.

Training alliances can also be made voluntarily, to equip apprentices with additional qualifications, which may go beyond the standard job profile. This can include for example training in e-skills (special computer programs), foreign languages, generic qualifications (soft skills).

In some federal states, institutionalized training alliances are formed (for example, the Upper Austria Company Training Alliance, and the Tirol Training Alliance). These offer the companies information and consultation on potential partner companies and educational institutions, and take over the task of coordinating measures for the training alliance.

FIGURE B3.17.1

Forms of training alliances and organizational options

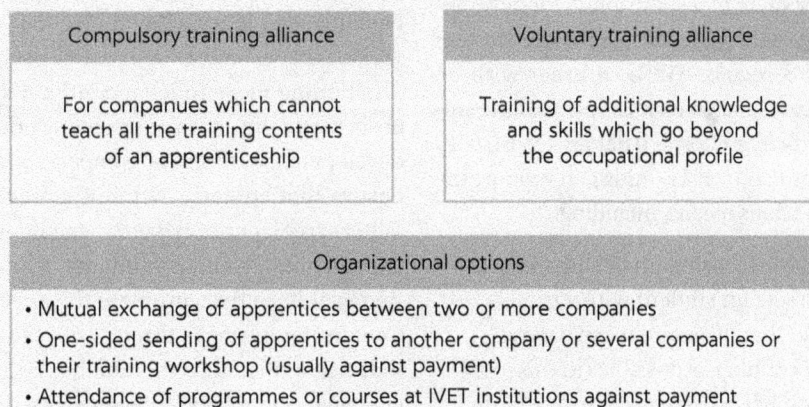

Compulsory training alliance	Voluntary training alliance
For companues which cannot teach all the training contents of an apprenticeship	Training of additional knowledge and skills which go beyond the occupational profile

Organizational options
• Mutual exchange of apprentices between two or more companies
• One-sided sending of apprentices to another company or several companies or their training workshop (usually against payment)
• Attendance of programmes or courses at IVET institutions against payment

Source: Federal Ministry of Economy, Family, and Youth 2014.

Sources: Petanovitsch, Schmid, and Bliem 2014; ReferNet 2014a.

BOX 3.18

Germany—models of firm collaboration to provide WBL

There are several collaborative training models in Germany which facilitate practical learning taking place in various firms, or in firm(s) and learning institutions:

1. *Leading enterprise with partner firm(s):* The leading company is the firm which is principally responsible for the overall apprenticeship. It concludes the training contract with the apprentice, pays the training allowance and organizes the temporary training periods itself or in the partner firm(s).
2. *Training by order.* Single training segments are awarded against cost reimbursement to other companies or training institutions.

Training association. Companies that provide certain sub-ranges of the prescribed training contents form an association, which takes on the overall organizational duties of a "training employer," while the individual firms under the association carry out the training.

3. *Syndicate.* Several companies take each trainees and exchange the trainees to agreed phases together.
4. *Joint venture.* A special form of collaborative training. In advance of the training period is a continuous change of the apprentice between several companies is a fix component during the course of the training.

Source: DualVet 2015.

BOX 3.19

Denmark—training centers

In 2013, the Danish government decided to establish 50 "Centers of Practical Training", to support VET students who are unable to obtain an internship within a reasonable time limit (2 months).

The Centers represent a new way of facilitating practical learning. Among others, vocational colleges now have a greater share of responsibility for developing a student's overall education plan if the student has not received a regular WBL contract with an employer. In this case, and when it is clear that the student has made sufficient efforts to obtain a WBL contract, the Center of Practical Training can support the student through various means, including:

- Facilitating the establishment of short term training contracts for student with various enterprises, so that the student can have as much in-firm training as possible (to this end, legislation has been revised to give more

flexibility to students who do not have a full contract with a company)
- Providing practical training in company-like surroundings.

Legislation allows a flexible approach to the organization of the Centers of Practical Training. They may be embedded in a single VET school, or work across various schools either as a part of a school network or functioning more independently. A strong focus on ensuring quality in training, among others through the development of teachers' competencies, is intended to ensure that students without a "regular, one-firm" WBL agreement receive the same level of practical experiences as those students who do. Moreover, financial incentives promote the effectiveness of the Centers, for example, through the use of performance indicators related to the number of apprenticeships agreements that the Centers manage.

Sources: ReferNet 2014b; Danish Ministry of Education website: http://www.emu.dk/modul/praktikcentre-organisationsformer;
Apprenticeship Toolbox, Funding Arrangements in Denmark: http://www.apprenticeship-toolbox.eu/index.php?option=com
_content&view=article&id=45:funding-arrangements-in-denmark&catid=34&Itemid=149.

Applications for Świętokrzyskie

Due to the current scarcity of work placements, the provision of practical learning outside of firms, by CPTs and VET schools, will likely remain relevant on the short term. As long as in-firm training opportunities remain limited, practical learning provided by CPTs and VET schools will be the only option for many VET students to acquire practical skills, and hence it can be considered justified to continue offering this opportunity. As WBL incidence and durations increase, the offer of practical learning options through CPTs and schools would be envisaged to (gradually) reduce.

However, for CPTs to promote—rather than discourage—WBL provision, their operating model needs to substantially move away from a sole focus on practical training provision, to one that emphasizes facilitating WBL. Depending on capacity, needs, and preferences, a variety of roles of the CPTs can be envisaged, ranging from serving as an intermediary between school and firms, to taking on a more substantive role in the management and organization of WBL, training in-firm instructors, and serving as a location for learning assessments. As this would entail in many cases a rather substantial change in operating approach of the CPTs, such changes would require substantial efforts from the CPTs managing authorities (the poviat government), likely accompanied by sufficient technical assistance to effectively achieve these changes.

CPTs are potentially well-placed to play an important role in the strengthening of WBL. Since CPTs have strong linkages with schools and (to an extent) with enterprises, they could in principle play a strong role in functioning as an intermediary to help identify WBL placements. For example, the practical training instructors at CPTs could not only be engaged in identifying appropriate WBL placements, but also potentially engage in activities such as WBL supervision and the training of in-firm instructors. CPTs could facilitate collaboration among firms in case students need placement in more than one enterprise to acquire all relevant skills through WBL (which is an activity that is already being carried out by the CPT in the Starachowice poviat), or help determine the appropriate mix of practical learning that will take place in-firm and in the CPT (figure 3.4).

Moreover, as long as CPTs continue to provide practical training, they should improve the relevance of training through strengthening the engagement of the private sector. One option to achieve this is to increase the extent to which the private sector determines the scope and content of training provision. While limited information is available on the manner in which CPTs currently determine their training offer, there generally appears to be ample room to improve

FIGURE 3.4

Possible roles of centers for practical training

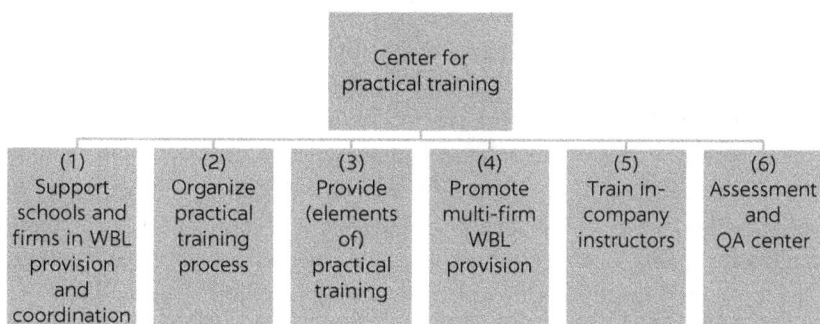

Source: World Bank.

their demand-responsiveness. This can be achieved, for example, through formalized mechanisms of consultation between the private sector and CPTs, or by including a strong private sector representation in the oversight and management of CPTs. Another option to strengthen private sector engagement is to increase its involvement in training provision, for example by inviting firm staff to provide guest lectures or to help design student assignments that reflect real-life problem solving activities.

CPTs can promote the acquisition of essential non-technical skills by increasing the extent to which CPT-training simulates the work environment. For example, project and team based assignments are likely to contribute to the acquisition of skills related to problem-solving, time management, and team work, which tend to be highly valued on the work floor and are less likely to be acquired when the focus of teaching is solely on equipping students with technical skills.

As the government plans to invest in substantially increasing the number of CPTs, it becomes even more important to ensure that CPTs play an appropriate role in facilitating WBL and providing demand-responsive training. As indicated in chapter 2 of this book, the government intends to establish CPTs in each of the country's *poviats*, which would increase the number of CPTs to 380 compared to the current 150. This makes it all the more important that CPTs contribute optimally, and in the most cost-efficient manner, to the achievement of appropriate learning outcomes by VET students. This would ideally imply the facilitation of quality work placements where possible, together with the development of quality and relative skills through direct training provision where WBL is not available or appropriate.

The ESF framework for VET provides ample scope to finance interventions to strengthen the role of CPTs in facilitating WBL. On the one hand, elements of the ESF framework promote the provision of practical learning activities in CPTs, via the use of performance indicators that measure the use of equipment in CPTs that has been purchased with EU funding. On the other hand, however, applicants for EU financing for VET are under no obligation to purchase equipment and the amount that may be spent on equipment is capped. Moreover, EU regulations also allow the use of funds for other activities that are more likely to promote WBL. For example, funding might be used for capacity-building and networking activities to improve cooperation with firms, reform CPT's institutional environment, and positioning the Center as the main institution coordinating WBL provision. The Partnership Agreement on ESF between the Government of Poland and the EC that is currently being renegotiated furthermore is likely to include a stronger focus on the promotion of WBL.

The pilot project on Implementation of Work-Based Learning in Świętokrzyskie will engage CPTs, and encourage where possible their role as facilitators of WBL. Depending on the implementation proposals that will emerge from the various *poviats* under the pilot project, it is expected that at least one to two CPTs will emerge as actors who will promote coordination and collaboration between VET schools and enterprises, and who may become actively engaged in areas such as in-firm instructor training or WBL supervision. Technical assistance that will be provided as part of the pilot project will be applied to support the CPTs in these roles. Lessons learned generated through the project on these aspects are expected to serve as input for the development of more appropriate and viable operating mechanisms for CPTs beyond the project implementation period.

NOTES

1. Largely due to the scope of the assistance that was provided under the Catching-Up Regions Initiative, this approach excluded a focus on aspects such as education pathways and career guidance, since these are dimensions that determine the quality of VET provision in general, and are not exclusively related to WBL.
2. Source: based on consultations at the regional level and with four local administrations (*poviats*).
3. Source: stakeholder consultations (May–October, 2016).
4. The European Training Foundation is an EU agency that helps transition and developing countries harness the potential of their human capital through the reform of education, training and labor market systems. See www.etf.europa.eu.
5. One example provided during consultations related to a firm which had agreed to host WBL students for a period of four weeks and had made arrangements accordingly, but subsequently the VET provider withdrew the students after one week without explanation.
6. Examples outside of Europe can be found among others in the Republic of Korea. An interesting approach there is a "supply chain approach," where larger enterprises support smaller firms that are part of their supply chain in training provision.
7. In the Polish terminology: the training is targeted at *practical training instructors* (firm employees) rather than at *practical training teachers* (teachers in VET schools).
8. This section applies a relatively broad definition of QA, not only related to "the systematic review of educational programs to ensure that acceptable standards of education, scholarship and infrastructure are being maintained" (definition by UNESCO), but also including additional approaches to enhance quality.
9. There were several accounts from the companies that they award highest grades based only on attendance or not being late to work.
10. For more details see https://www.qibb.at/de/english.html.
11. As described in chapter 2, ambiguities in the regulations allow for different interpretations on whether or not traineeships are required to take place in firms. However, most stakeholders consulted interpret the legislation as requiring traineeships to be firm-based.
12. One of the ESF indicators measures the "number of VET schools and providers using equipment purchased from EFS funds."

REFERENCES

BIBB. 2014. *Vocational Training Regulations and the Process behind Them.* Bonn, Germany.

CEDEFOP. 2012. "Vocational Education and Training in Denmark. Short Description." Cedefop Research Paper 37. Publications Office. Luxembourg city, Luxembourg.

Danish Ministry of Education. 2000. *New Structure of the Danish Vocational Education and Training System* (accessed 22 March 2017), Copenhagen, Denmark. http://static.uvm.dk /publikationer/2000/newstructure/hel.htm.

DualVet. 2015. *Dual VET System. Transfer of Successful Structures and Guidance for Implementing the Dual VET System. Training Company Trainers.* Chamber of Commerce, Industry and Services from Zaragoza, Zaragoza, Spain.

EQAVET. 2012. *Quality Assuring Work-Based Learning.* European Quality Assurance for VET. Dublin, Ireland.

ETF (European Training Foundation). 2014. *Work-Based Learning: A Handbook for Policy Makers and Social Partners in ETF Partner Countries.* European Training Foundation. Torino, Italy.

European Commission. 2013. *Work-Based Learning in Europe. Practices and Policy Pointers.* European Commission. Brussels, Belgium.

———. 2015. *High-Performing Apprenticeships and Work-Based Learning—20 Guiding Principles.* European Commission, DG Employment. Brussels, Belgium.

Federal Ministry of Economy, Family and Youth. 2014. *Apprenticeship. Dual Vocational Education and Training in Austria. Modern Training with a Future.* Ministry of Economy, Family and Youth. Vienna, Austria.

Kis, V. 2016. *Work, Train, Win: Work-Based Learning Design and Management for Productivity Gains.*

Kuczera, M. 2017. "Incentives for Apprenticeship." OECD Education Working Paper 152, OECD Publishing. Paris, France.

Lammi, Anne. 2014. *Guide on Implementing Workplace Instructor Training.* Finnish National Board of Education. Tampere, Finland.

Petanovitsch, Alexander, Schmid Kurt, and Bliem Wolfgang. 2014. *Success Factors for the Dual Training. Possibilities of Transfer.* Business Development Institute of the Austrian Federal Economic Chamber (WIFI). Vienna, Austria.

ReferNet. 2014a. *Apprenticeship-Type Schemes and Structured Work-Based Learning Programmes* Institut für Bildungsforschung der Wirtschaft. Vienna, Austria.

——. 2014b. *Apprenticeship-Type Schemes and Structured Work-Based Learning Programmes. Denmark.* Metropolitan University College/Danish National Center for Development of Vocational Education and Training. Copenhagen, Denmark.

——. 2014c. *Apprenticeship-Type Schemes and Structured Work-Based Learning Programmes. Norway.* The Norwegian Directorate for Education and Training. Oslo, Norway.

——. 2014d. *Apprenticeship-Type Schemes and Structured Work-Based Learning Programmes. The Netherlands.* Expertisecentrum Beroepsonderwijs (ecbo). 'S Hertogenbosch, the Netherlands.

Tarja, Frisk, ed. 2014. *Guide for the Implementation of Vocational Teacher' Work Placement Periods.* Finnish National Board of Education. Tampere, Finland.

4 Recommendations, Next Steps, and Lessons Learned

The first section of this chapter presents recommendations for strengthening WBL in technical education in Świętokrzyskie. The recommendations are based on the current context in the region, the WBL analytical-framework, and the relevant international practices as described in the previous chapters of this book. The second section will describe the concrete next steps that the region is taking to strengthen WBL through a pilot project that is expected to be financed by the European Social Fund. Lastly, the third section describes lessons learned from the technical assistance that was provided in Poland that can usefully be taken into account when carrying out similar exercises in other contexts where a transition from a mostly school-based to a more enterprise-based vocational education and training (VET) provision is considered; this last section will discuss both lessons learned related to the process of identifying appropriate reforms and interventions, and related to interventions that may have the highest likelihood of success.

RECOMMENDATIONS FOR STRENGTHENING WBL IN TECHNICAL EDUCATION IN ŚWIĘTOKRZYSKIE

Technical education in Świętokrzyskie (as in all of Poland) remains largely school-based, due to weaknesses in nearly all dimensions that were identified to matter for strong WBL provision. The overarching constraints relate to weak incentives and capacity among all key stakeholders, especially among schools, firms, and Centers for Practical Training (CPTs). This results in a situation where the incidence, duration, and quality of WBL are generally weak, and effective concerted efforts to remedy this situation are few and far between. While not the explicit focus of this book, limitations related to incentives and capacity may have an impact beyond the scope of WBL: the public VET system has limited incentives and capacity to respond to the requirements of employers, and (therefore) employers have limited incentives to invest in working with a public VET system which they find unresponsive to their needs.

A multi-pronged, pragmatic approach is recommended to strengthen WBL provision in the Świętokrzyskie region. Such an approach would tackle important constraints to WBL provision simultaneously, in a manner that aims to generate relatively quick results. In particular, the recommended approach is as follows:

- **Apply a comprehensive approach, simultaneously targeting all key dimensions to WBL provision that are intertwined and mutually reinforcing.** The current context can be described as a "vicious circle of constraints." The justification for a comprehensive approach is that addressing several key challenges creates the possibility of changing this into a "virtuous circle," where progress in one area will boost the positive impact of activities in others. For example, increased incentives for WBL participation are expected to boost stakeholders' interest in engaging in coordination platforms, which in turn would promote the establishment of mechanisms to support WBL, which would incentivize actors to engage in WBL implementation, etc.
- **Apply a pragmatic approach and initially facilitate WBL participation of those firms and VET providers that show the highest motivation and at least a minimum level of capacity.** The justification of this approach is that it is expected to increase the likelihood of being able to showcase early success. In practice, this approach may imply that in the early stages of WBL implementation, participating stakeholders will be concentrated among larger-size and more competitive firms, better-managed VET providers, and higher performing students for which there is relatively strong demand on the labor market. It is also possible that initiatives emerge that include participants who may be considered harder to reach, such as smaller-size enterprises, or firms that are willing and able to cater to students with special needs.[1] Particular incentives and assistance could be directed to such initiatives, to ensure that while the support system for WBL implementation develops, mechanisms targeting these groups are incorporated from the start.

Taking into account the above proposed approach, a range of specific recommendations were developed to strengthen the incidence, duration and quality of WBL in technical education. While particularly developed for the Świętokrzyskie region, where employment outcomes and economic dynamism tend to be weaker than in most other regions of Poland, the recommendations are to a substantial extent considered to be applicable nation-wide. The recommendations are summarized below, starting with those that require national-level interventions, and following with those that can be initiated at the regional level. While the regional-level interventions can be implemented without additional national-level reforms, it is expected that their positive impact would be reinforced if national-level interventions would be carried out as well.

Recommendations for interventions at the national level

1. Adapt the VET regulatory framework to clarify regulations, increase incentives, and introduce quality assurance mechanisms. In particular, revisions are proposed that would:
   - *Clarify definitions* and provisions that currently lead to ambiguities and misinterpretations, such as whether the requirement to provide traineeships in "real working conditions" refers exclusively to in-firm learning

experiences, and related to the difference between practical activities and traineeships (which may be superfluous)

- *Increase incentives* for VET providers and their managing bodies to engage in WBL by increasing the minimum requirements for the share of learning that is to take place in firms[2]
- Introduce clear mechanisms and procedures to assure the quality and relevance of WBL including, among others, related to identifying and assessing learning outcomes.

The above regulatory changes may need to be accompanied, at least in their initial stages, by support measures to VET schools and other stakeholders, to ensure their awareness of the changes as well as their ability to comply with them.

2. Adapt the accountability and governance framework to increase incentives for engagement in WBL. In addition to adapting the regulatory framework, further national-level interventions could be considered to strengthen WBL implementation. These could, include introducing performance-based elements in accountability and financing mechanisms, which may likely need to be preceded by activities to strengthen monitoring and evaluation mechanisms. Similar to revising the regulatory framework, such reforms may potentially need to be accompanied by support measures to VET providers and other stakeholders, to ensure that they have the desired impact. After all, increased accountability and results-based financing will only have the desired impact when providers are able to meet performance requirements.

Recommendations for interventions at the regional level

3. At the initial stage, investing in promoting coordination between (groups of) schools and firms may take precedence over facilitating higher-level, regional coordination mechanisms. WBL requires collaboration between employers and schools, and a pragmatic approach may be to focus initial attention on fostering such partnerships at a small and local level. Broader, regional coordination and consultation platforms can, eventually, provide essential direction to individual VET providers and firms in providing effective WBL (and relevant VET in general). Such platforms would generate economies of scale in coordination, and would ideally include activities that are unlikely to be carried out by smaller groups of stakeholder, such as for example developing and disseminating sound regional or local VET strategies that are based on relevant labor market information. However, international experience shows that efforts to establish such more strategic-level coordination mechanisms are not always successful; when incentives and capacity are lacking among key stakeholders, such platforms may be short-lived or end up existing only "on paper," without being effective in practice. For Świętokrzyskie, the recommendation is therefore to apply a gradual approach to promoting stakeholder coordination, starting with the facilitation of effective coordination and collaboration between a limited number of schools and firms which show particular and concrete interest in implementing WBL. Building on these experiences, broader and more formalized coordination mechanisms (such as through sector skills councils) could be foreseen at a later stage.

4. Address weak incentives and capacity with a well-balanced package of financial and technical support for all key stakeholders. International practices show that strong support structures are in place in those countries that implement a sound WBL mechanism. Particularly in contexts where VET provision is still largely school-based, such as in Poland, the availability of effective support is even more important to facilitate the transition to increased WBL. The following broad principles are recommended to apply when determining the exact scope and nature of support:

- **Include all essential stakeholders:** effective WBL implementation depends on the willingness and capacity of both firms and VET providers and, to a somewhat lesser extent, CPTs. Support measures therefore need to include all these stakeholders. Ensuring incentives and capacity of VET providers, but not of firms (or vice versa) is unlikely to generate the desired impact

- **Provide an appropriate mix of technical and financial support:** technical support builds capacity and reduces the (transaction) costs of implementing WBL; financial support further improves incentives for participation in WBL. While it is recognized that financial compensation may be needed, especially as employers are starting to gain experience with WBL implementation, there are various reasons to apply a cautious approach in using financing as a means to incentivize firm participation in WBL. Among others, international evidence shows that its impact may be modest (Kuczera 2017). Moreover, employers who participate in WBL because they recognize the benefits of students' contribution to production and of being able to recruit well-trained graduates, are more likely to be willing to engage in effort to ensure high quality WBL. Conversely, if the main incentives of employers to engage in WBL are related to the financial compensation, then they might only want to provide minimum input in ensuring the quality of WBL

- **Tailor technical support to stakeholder needs:** sound stakeholder consultations should inform both the scope and the delivery methods of the technical support that will be offered

- **When determining the level of financial support, consider that stakeholders may require more substantial financial support during the "transition period" than in a mature WBL system, since:**
  - In a mature WBL system, VET providers will have adjusted their human resource planning to ensure that sufficient staff can allocate time to supporting WBL. During the transition period, providers may need to (temporarily) recruit additional staff with the appropriate skills
  - Both the real and perceived cost-benefit ratio of firms participating in WBL is higher than in a mature system, because (a) it may take some time for firms to acknowledge the long-term benefits of WBL; (b) the actual immediate benefits of WBL for firms may initially be relatively low, as firms may only gradually learn how to ensure the contribution of WBL-students in their production processes; (c) costs of WBL will initially be relatively high, as it will take some time for firms to develop the most efficient way to guide students during their WBL experience

- **Consider the broader implications of transitioning from a school-based system for VET providers.** Substantially strengthening the provision of VET through WBL comprises a significant systems' change, with potentially relatively strong implications for, particularly, VET schools and CPTs. Support provided should acknowledge the need for appropriate change management which could include, for example, reallocating and training teaching staff so that they can be effectively engaged in WBL implementation, and training teaching staff to ensure that they are up to date with the production processes and skills requirements in firms that offer WBL places.

5. Support stakeholders with the implementation of sound quality assurance mechanisms without creating additional barriers for engaging in WBL. Feasible and appropriate quality assurance (QA) approaches are considered to be those that can be implemented taking into account the limited capacity and resources of stakeholders, and that are not so stringent and time-consuming that they discourage stakeholders (especially enterprises) from engaging in WBL. Over time, as capacity and incentives for WBL implementation increase among stakeholders, QA mechanisms can be added or strengthened to gradually arrive at an overall system that inspires a sufficient level of confidence among all relevant actors about the quality and relevance of WBL (and overall VET) provision.

6. Adapt the operating model and improve the demand-responsiveness of training provision through Centers of Practical Training. Whereas in other countries workshops and laboratories that simulate work-environments are considered a second-best option compared to in-firm training, this does not appear to be the case in Świętokrzyskie, where in some cases they seem to be the default option for practical learning. While this is likely partly the result of the limited incidence of in-firm training in the region, the existence and operations of workshops and laboratories in schools and CPT appear also to contribute to the low incidence of in-firm training. A revised operating model with objectives, procedures, and incentives that are geared to promoting in-firm training and applying work place simulations only when needed, and which more explicitly and effectively take into account the need to provide demand-response skill development activities (for example by giving the private sector a stronger role in their management), could greatly improve the extent to which these actors contribute to the acquisition of relevant skills by VET students. An option to consider would be to engage CPTs in consultation or capacity building activities that are described above.

NEXT STEPS: THE ŚWIĘTOKRZYSKIE PILOT PROJECT TO STRENGTHEN WBL IN TECHNICAL EDUCATION

Objectives of the pilot project

Supported by the technical assistance provided through the Catching-Up Regions Initiative, the Marshal Office of the Świętokrzyskie voivodship in collaboration with key stakeholders designed a pilot project to strengthen WBL. The project is expected to be financed by the ESF in the framework of the Operational Program Knowledge Education Development (OP KED) as a social innovation, and will be implemented during the period 2017–20.

The project's objective is to pilot a variety of approaches to promote the incidence, duration, and quality of WBL, based on the knowledge generated through the technical assistance initiative. The project will target WBL provision to students of technical education as an integral part of the formal VET program, with the ultimate objective of improving the employability of VET graduates. In addition to strengthening VET implementation in Świętokrzyskie during the project implementation period, the project is expected to generate lessons learned that will serve to inform further interventions to strengthen WBL after 2020, both in Świętokrzyskie and in other regions in Poland.

Grant-selection criteria

Under the project, a grant mechanism will be established to provide financing to local stakeholders who develop viable pilot approaches for WBL implementation which meet a number of selection criteria. Among others, these criteria will concern:

- Requirements related to the identification of the stakeholders who will be involved in grant implementation. In particular, each grant application needs to be supported by at least one VET school and at least one firm as implementing partners. With this approach, the pilot project will only support initiatives where WBL-places have already been identified, thus avoiding the challenge of the "school-first approach" in which the identification of work placements can be a challenging and time-consuming task.[3] Proposals that involve several employers and firms as implementing partners will be prioritized
- The establishment of clear and adequate coordination mechanisms among, particularly, the implementing partners, as well as with social partners and local authorities
- The number of hours that students will engage in in-firm learning activities. The minimum requirement that students need to spend on WBL is 50 percent of the required number of hours for practical activities
- The clear identification of WBL learning outcomes
- The application of quality assurance measures that are based on clear procedures describing, among others, the key aspects of WBL provision that are expected to contribute to the achievement of appropriate learning outcomes (such as for example the competencies of in-company trainers) and that will be subject to QA reviews; the process with which these elements will be assessed; and the division of QA responsibilities between VET providers, firms, and students and
- The expected (financial) sustainability of implementation arrangements beyond the implementation period of the Pilot Project.

Strengthening capacity and incentives of firms and schools

Employers will be supported through a mix of capacity building and financial incentives. Capacity building will include the provision of information and advisory services on a range of subjects, including on the general aspects of WBL (regulations, benefits, costs, etc.); on effective coordination and collaboration with VET schools; and on organizing WBL taking into account the specific context of the firm (e.g., related to facilitating the contribution of WBL-students to production processes, ensuring compliance with health and safety regulations; developing learning plans; and quality assurance of WBL); ensuring smooth communication with schools). In addition to these advisory services, the pilot project will provide the necessary pedagogical training for workplace instructors. Financial compensation will be made available to employers to cover the costs of instructors, training materials, work wear for students and, where justified, equipment for workstations for WBL students.

Similarly, VET schools and CPTs participating in the pilot project will be offered capacity building support as well as financing to compensate for the costs associated with organizing WBL provision. Advisory services that will be available for schools will include guidance on identifying and maintaining a constructive relationship with employers offering work placements; assistance on determining WBL learning objectives and assessing the learning outcomes of WBL; and support in the design and organization of the school-based part of VET provision, taking into account that students will spend less time in the school and that the school-based content will be reduced. In addition, schools will be eligible to receive financial support to cover the costs of human resources that need to be allocated to the organization and administration of WBL.

Additional financial support will be made available to cover the costs of student participation in WBL. This is expected to include the costs of health and safety training, the medical examination that is required before embarking on WBL, transport and accommodation, and potentially additional remuneration.

For each pilot under the project, one of the implementing partners will serve as a "grant champion" that—assisted by the external advisory services provider—will take responsibility for coordinating the support activities that will be provided to all participating firms and schools. The grant champion is expected to be either a participating school or firm, or a CPT that is involved in WBL implementation. Together with the external advisory services provider, the grant champion will ensure smooth implementation and provide support services to all actors that are engaged in the implementation of the pilot project.

Management of the pilot project

The pilot project will be managed by the regional authorities (Marshall Office), which has taken a leading role in promoting WBL in the region. Among others, the Marshall Office will be responsible for providing information and guidance to potential grant applicants; organize calls for grant proposals; manage the evaluation and selection of grant proposals; and monitor their implementation. The Marshal Office will also contract the external advisory services provider, which will consist of one or more experts with extensive experience in WBL implementation. Once lessons learned from the implementation of the pilot project have emerged, the Marshall Office is also expected to engage in the active promotion of good practices, and encourage their adaptation by other actors within and outside of the region.

Generating lessons learned

Several aspects of the design of the pilot project will help to ensure that the lessons learned generated through the pilots can feed into future activities to strengthen WBL in Świętokrzyskie and beyond. First, the templates and other guidance material that will be developed through the project are expected to facilitate stakeholders who implement WBL beyond the direct grant beneficiaries. Second, with the support of the advisory services provider that will be procured by the Marshal Office, a sound monitoring and evaluation mechanism will ensure that the strengths and weaknesses of the various approaches that will be implemented are recorded, and can be readily disseminated. One of the focus areas of measurement will be the employability of students who benefit from the project, compared to that of an appropriately identified control group ("direct impact").[4] In addition, a qualitative approach will be applied to assess improvements in institutional capacity of key

TABLE 4.1 **Addressing key dimensions for strengthening WBL through the pilot project**

KEY DIMENSION	ACTIVITIES UNDER THE PILOT PROJECT
1. Appropriate governance and financing framework	As the pilot project is a regional project, it will not address constraints that require national-level interventions
2. Effective mechanisms for stakeholder consultation and coordination	• Initiate collaboration and coordination between participating VET providers and firms, associated local governments, and the regional government • Engage additional stakeholders who may play a leading role in coordination and consultation activities in the future • Recording of lessons learned and good practices
3. Adequate incentives and capacity of VET providers	• Financing for WBL implementation • Capacity building on WBL implementation, for example, on interacting with firms, adapting curricula to incorporate WBL, monitoring WBL placements, and teacher development • Development of templates and guidance material on critical elements of WBL implementation • Recording of lessons learned and good practices
4. Adequate incentives and capacity of firms	• Financing for WBL implementation • Capacity building on WBL implementation, for example, on interacting with schools, engaging students in production processes, in-firm instructor training, and quality assurance • Development of templates and guidance material on critical elements of WBL implementation • Recording of lessons learned and good practices
5. Quality assurance mechanisms for WBL	• Capacity building on QA for firms and schools • Development of templates and guidance material on relevant QA approaches • Recording of lessons learned and good practices
6. A facilitating role for Centers for Practical Training	• Capacity building of CPTs which participate in the pilot project, including particularly on CPTs' potential facilitating role in WBL implementation, and aligning CPT training provision with WBL activities and, more generally, labor demand • Recording of lessons learned and good practices

Source: Based on draft description of pilot project on implementation of work-based learning in Świętokrzyskie 2017-23 (March, 2017).
Note: WBL = work-based learning; VET = Vocational education and training; CPT = Center for Practical Training; QA = Quality assurance.

stakeholders, as a measure of the extent to which the project facilitates effective WBL provision beyond the project implementation project ("indirect impact"). Third, to lay the groundworks for the establishment of a structural coordination and support mechanism to facility WBL implementation in the future, relevant stakeholders beyond the direct grant beneficiaries will be invited to engage in the implementation and monitoring of the pilot project; these will particularly include the regional labor market council, and possibly actors such as the VET cluster of the SEZ and employer representatives, depending on their preferences and capacity.

The pilot project will address the majority of the dimensions that have been identified to be key to strengthening WBL in technical education. The exception is the dimension related to the governance and financing framework, as addressing this dimension requires national level reforms that are beyond the scope of the regional pilot project. The way in which each dimension is addressed through the pilot project is summarized in table 4.1

LESSONS LEARNED FOR STRENGTHENING WBL IN A SCHOOL-BASED VET SYSTEM

Activities under the technical assistance initiative targeted at strengthening WBL in Świętokrzyskie have generated various lessons learned that may be usefully applied in other contexts where stakeholders consider analyses and interventions to promote WBL. These lessons are summarized below, categorized by those relating to the analysis of strengths and weaknesses for WBL implementation, and those related to the design of interventions. These lessons could be considered in concert with and complementary to the policy lessons on strengthening WBL as developed by the ETF (appendix B). As at the time of writing of this book, the implementation of the Świętokrzyskie pilot project was yet to commence, no information is provided on implementation aspects and results of this project.

Analyzing the strengths and challenges for WBL implementation

- **Perform a sound analysis of the strengths and weaknesses of the current system for WBL provision, using a combination of regulatory and literature review and stakeholder consultations**. The analytical framework developed by the European Commission (European Commission 2015) proved a useful basis for the analysis in Świętokrzyskie. As the use of this framework highlighted the large number of diverse challenges faced in the region, the "twenty dimensions" for WBL implementation that are identified in this framework were reduced to six priority dimensions for the region, which was considered to be a more manageable number on which to base the further analysis.
- **Include in the analysis a review of incentives and constraints for WBL implementation of schools and other public sector stakeholders**. While extensive literature exists on approaches to incentivize and support employers, students, and stakeholder coordination, substantially less information is available that focuses on VET schools and other public sector stakeholders. Nevertheless, particularly in a context where VET provision is still largely supply-driven and school-based, these stakeholders may face considerable constraints to introducing stronger WBL elements in training provision in terms of their capacity and—perhaps more importantly—incentives to implement reforms.
- **Incentives and capacity of all stakeholders may be the crucial underlying determinants of effective WBL implementation.** The incidence, duration, and quality of WBL ultimately depends on stakeholders' motivation and ability to forge effective partnerships, offer work placements, adjust training programs to accommodate in-firm learning, and assure the quality and relevance of students WBL experiences. In a system which is predominantly school-based, incentives and capacity are mostly lacking, which is an important issue that requires to be addressed to promote effective WBL.

Designing interventions to promote WBL implementation

- **Recognize that introducing substantial elements of WBL in a largely school-based system entails a significant systems' change which will have strong implications for both VET providers and firms.** Transitioning from a school-based system to, for example, apprenticeship systems that are present in some other EU member states or that exist in basic vocational education in Poland, is likely to require both time and extensive efforts to ensure that all key aspects to promote WBL provision— ranging from an appropriate regulatory and governance framework to the

presence of effective support mechanisms for individual stakeholders—
are sufficiently in place.

- **Successful reforms to strengthen WBL may require one or more "champions" to trigger and sustain the process.** The transition to more WBL-based VET may require the leadership form at least one key actor (or group of actors) to bring stakeholder together. While it is clear that many stakeholders need to be involved in strengthening WBL provision, it can be less obvious who this "WBL champion" could be, especially in a context where private sector organization may be relatively weak, and school incentives are insufficiently geared toward promoting WBL. In Świętokrzyskie, the regional authorities have emerged as a WBL champion, including by ensuring that the technical assistance under the Catching-Up Regions Program was directed, among others, to promoting WBL. This technical assistance, subsequently, is considered to have increased both incentives and capacity among key stakeholders, including the regional authorities, employers, schools, CPTs and local governments.

- **When multiple challenges for WBL implementation exist, they might be mutually enforcing and may therefore be best addressed simultaneously.** As described earlier in this chapter, different constraints to WBL may exacerbate each other. Therefore, an approach that addresses them simultaneously, may contribute to turning a vicious circle of constraints into a virtuous circle where improvements in one dimension (such as school capacity) may trigger enhancements in others (such as employer incentives to offer work placements).

- **International approaches to facilitate WBL implementation should be adapted to fit the local context.** Existing literature on promoting WBL, especially when relating to the European context, tends to have a strong focus on apprenticeships, often (although not always) in countries where there have been in place for a long time. Technical education in Świętokrzyskie, however, is still largely school-based, and the technical assistance activities focused on strengthening work placements, rather than on introducing more extensive apprenticeship-type mechanisms. This, particularly, implied that some of the international approaches that were reviewed, were either considered to be inappropriate or not feasible for immediate implementation. For example, administratively heavy approaches to accrediting employers prior to their engagement in WBL were considered too elaborate for the relatively modest duration of WBL placements that are envisaged (at least in the shorter term) in the region; and a self-evaluation approach such as is applied for example in Switzerland, appears a more appropriate mechanism to apply to assess firm readiness for WBL participation. Similarly, considering the still rather weak coordination among social partners in the region, approaches that in other countries are managed or led by them (such as the monitoring of WBL performance in Austria), may in Świętokrzyskie be better implemented with stronger engagement from other stakeholders (such as the regional Marshal Office during implementation of the pilot project.

- **Ensure sound monitoring and evaluation of the progress and impact of interventions.** The need to monitor and evaluate interventions should be considered from the project design-stage, to ensure that baselines and control groups are timely identified, and progress and impact can be adequately tracked. Moreover, intermediate performance indicators measuring increases in stakeholder capacity can be a useful addition to output indicators related to the quality, incidence, and/or relevance of WBL, and outcome indicators including graduate employability and employer satisfaction with graduates' skills. When transitioning to a VET approach that includes stronger WBL, improvements in stakeholder capacity—especially of firms and schools—can be especially appropriate since it may take some time before concrete improvements in gradate employability and employer satisfaction can be measured. The Świętokrzyskie pilot project, for example, includes capacity-related indicators that will be measured through a qualitative approach.

NOTES

1. While it is regularly presumed that smaller-sized enterprises are relatively hard to reach for WBL engagement, there are international examples of intensive participation by smaller firms. See for example, IBW (2016). Also in Poland, apprentices in basic vocational education are mostly employed by smaller sized crafts enterprises.

2. Setting a clear minimum may promote employer engagement and result in WBL implementation even in excess of the minimum requirements. For example, the Dutch school-based upper secondary VET system requires a minimum of 20 percent of study time spent on the job, and typically the actual share is around 30 percent (Vrieze et al. 2009).

3. See chapter 1 for a description of the "school-first" and "employer-first" approaches. The prerequisite to identify employer-firm partnerships has similarities with approaches applied, among others, in higher VET in Sweden and by the Competency Based Training Fund in Barbados (on the latter, see: https://blogs.iadb.org/education/2016/06/03/barbados-training-technical/).

4. Employment outcomes should ideally be measured some time (e.g., six months) after students graduate. Due to the duration of the project implementation period, the project's impact on graduate employability can only be measured after the project has been completed. The Świętokrzyskie Marshal's Office has committed to ensuring continued evaluation activities beyond the project implementation period for this purpose.

REFERENCES

European Commission. 2015. *High-Performing Apprenticeships and Work-Based Learning—20 Guiding Principles*. European Commission, DG Employment. Brussels, Belgium.

Kuczera, M. 2017. "Incentives for Apprenticeship." OECD Education Working Paper 152, OECD Publishing. Paris, France.

Vrieze, G., J. van Kuijk, and J. de Loo. 2009. *Tijd voor beroepspraktijkvorming en andere onderwijsactiviteiten*. ITS, Radboud University. Nijmegen, the Netherlands.

Appendix A
Stakeholder Consultations

TABLE A.1 Regional working group meetings (May–September 2016)

PUBLIC AUTHORITIES

1. Świętokrzyskie Marshal's office
2. Starachowice Poviat office
3. Educational superintendent's office

VET PROVIDERS

1. Transport and Mechatronics Scool Complex in Skarżysko-Kamienna
2. School Complex No 3 in Ostrowiec Świętokrzyski
3. Vocational School Complex No 3 in Starachowice
4. H. Chrzanowska Post-Secondary Medical School in Morawica
5. Center for Practical Training in Kielce

OTHER INSTITUTIONS

1. CELSA Huta Ostrowiec
2. Lewiatan Private Employers' Association
3. Staropolska Chamber of Industry and Commerce
4. Regional labor office
5. Świętokrzyskie Teachers' Development Center
6. Świętokrzyskie Voluntary Labor Corps
7. Starachowice special economic zone
8. Jan Kochanowski University in Kielce
9. Świętokrzyskie University of Technology
10. Starachowice special economic zone

TABLE A.2 **Individual consultations (June–October 2016)**

PUBLIC AUTHORITIES—POVIAT OFFICES
1. Końskie
2. Ostrowiec Świętokrzyski
3. Skarżysko-Kamienna
4. Starachowice

VET PROVIDERS
1. Vocational School Complex No 1 in Końskie
2. Vocational School Complex No 2 in Końskie
3. Vocational School Complex No 1 in Ostrowiec Świętokrzyski
4. Vocational School Complex No 3 in Ostrowiec Świętokrzyski
5. Center for Vocational and Continuing Training in Ostrowiec Świętokrzyski
6. Economic School Complex in Skarżysko-Kamienna
7. Technical School Complex in Skarżysko-Kamienna
8. Vocational School Complex No 1 in Starachowice
9. Vocational School Complex No 2 in Starachowice
10. Vocational School Complex No 3 in Starachowice
11. Center for Practical Training in Kielce
12. Center for Practical Training in Starachowice

COMPANIES
1. Animex (Starachowice)
2. CELSA Huta Ostrowiec
3. MAN Bus (Starachowice)
4. NSK Bearings (Kielce)
5. Perfopol (Starachowice)
6. RR Donneley (Starachowice)
7. Starpol (Starachowice)

OTHER INSTITUTIONS
1. Chamber of Crafts in Ostrowiec Świętokrzyski
2. Special economic zone in Starachowice

TABLE A.3 **Group workshops on preparation of pilot project proposal (December 2016–January 2017)**

PUBLIC AUTHORITIES
1. Poviat Authority Starachowice
2. Poviat Authority Skarżysko-Kamienna
3. Poviat Authority Sandomierz
4. Local employment office in Starachowice
5. Local employment office in Skrażysko-Kamienna
6. Marshal office

continued

TABLE A.3, *continued*

VET PROVIDERS

1. Economic School Complex in Skarżysko-Kamienna
2. Technical School Complex in Skarżysko-Kamienna
3. Technical School Complex no 4 in Skarżysko-Kamienna
4. Complex of School of Railway and Mechanics in Skarżysko-Kamienna
5. Vocational School Complex No 2 in Starachowice
6. Vocational School Complex No 3 in Starachowice
7. Vocational School Complex No 1 in Starachowice
8. Economic School Complex in Skarżysko-Kamienna
9. School Complex in Suchedniów
10. Centrum of Practical Education Starachowice
11. Centrum of Practical Education Skarżysko

COMPANIES

1. ZSK
2. ZSTM Skarżysko
3. Mesko S.A.
4. ZME Zamel
5. Animex Foods Sp. z o.o.
6. PKP PL S.A.
7. Hairdresser in Skarżysko
8. TV Starachowice
9. LSC Communication
10. Gerda Sp. z o.o. Starachowice
11. Odlewnie Polskie S.A.
12. ZPHU ELRUZ
13. Klinika Komputera
14. PKC Group Poland
15. Termatex

OTHER INSTITUTIONS

1. Special Economic Zone Starachowice
2. Voluntary Labor Corps

Appendix B
Policy Lessons on Strengthening Work-Based Learning (ETF)

In its publication *Work-Based Learning. A Handbook for Policy Makers and Social Partners in ETF Partner Countries* (2014), the European Training Foundation identifies the following policy lessons for countries that want to introduce, expand or reform work-based learning systems or programs (pp. 32–33)

1. **Start with a shared vision**, involve key stakeholders in developing it, and make sure that all key stakeholders are committed to it. This should include as a minimum all relevant government ministries and agencies, employer organizations, chambers (of commerce, trade, craft, agriculture, etc.), employee organizations and vocational education and training (VET) providers. Local and regional economic development bodies, parents, community organizations and non-governmental organizations are other stakeholders in many countries

2. **Build a policy framework around this shared vision**, and ensure that it has strong political support

3. **Make sure that the framework gives strong ownership and control to the social partners** over key parts of the new system or program. This could include elements such as policy development, selecting participants, developing skill standards, developing the curriculum, assessment and certification, and quality assurance

4. **Make sure that the framework includes proposals for financing** (this may include wages, subsidies, taxes, industry levies, social security and insurance, and other similar factors) that will motivate both employers and learners to participate

5. **Create a comprehensive legislative and regulatory framework** to support the policy framework and vision. Make sure that the legislative and regulatory framework clearly sets out the areas of responsibility of each of the key stakeholders

6. **Create channels for institutional coordination and communication t**o support the framework, such as national VET councils, industry-sector councils and regional councils

7. **Make sure that new systems or programs do not compete** (for participants, for employer places, or for the involvement of social partners) with existing systems or programs of work-based learning. If there is more than one type of work-based learning program (for example, apprenticeships and internships), make sure that they target different occupations, industries or individuals

8. **Take a long-term view.** Unless there exists a strong institutional tradition that is likely to support work-based learning programs and systems, **begin with pilot programs.** Evaluate and learn from these, share what has been learned with key stakeholders, and modify and improve what is being done as a result of experience and evaluations

9. **Use international partnerships** to help build the system if the necessary knowledge and experience is not available nationally

10. **Put a great deal of effort into building the tools** that are needed to support new programs and systems, including competency standards, curricula, skill lists for enterprises and students, and assessment tools

11. **Put a great deal of effort into developing the knowledge and skills** of the people who will need to make the system or program work at the local level: enterprise tutors or trainers, vocational teachers, curriculum developers and social partners

12. **Actively market and communicate the new system** or programs to all key stakeholders. Do this at the local and regional levels, not just at the national level.